IN BUSINESS WITH YOURSELF

IN BUSINESS WITH YOURSELF

Understanding Your Identity to Make or Break Your Business

Michelle Lestas

The Executive Identity Model ®

ORPEN PRESS

Published by
Orpen Press
Upper Floor, Unit B3
Hume Centre
Hume Avenue
Park West Industrial Estate
Dublin 12
Ireland

email: info@orpenpress.com
www.orpenpress.com

Paperback ISBN 978-1-78605-113-4
ePub ISBN 978-1-78605-114-1

Printed in Dublin by SPRINTprint Ltd

To my husband Nicholas, my soulmate for over 33 years, who has steadied me in storms and swam with me in calm waters

To my wonderfully talented and beautiful sons, Finn and Aron, who bring nothing but colour to my life

To my Dad, John, and Mum, Pat — forever my mentors, even now as they sleep

ACKNOWLEDGEMENTS

There are so many people who have helped me to get to this place and to you I am forever grateful – you know who you are. There are a few particular people I also want to single out for a mention. Firstly, to all the business leaders I have worked with over the years, who actively engaged in my suggestions and methods; without your honesty this book would not have been possible. To Orpen Press and particularly Eileen O'Brien and David McCartney, who showed their faith in me, making this publication a reality. Finally, to my husband, Nicholas (@Nikosart), who was able to capture the 'eight identities' so beautifully through his painting on the front cover.

CONTENTS

AUTHOR'S NOTE

The content of this book is based on my experience, knowledge and observations of business and organisational leadership gathered over 25 years. I grew up in a family business and after a couple of CEO positions and undertaking a Masters in Business Administration, I set up a management consultancy business in 2000. I have worked as a business advisor for 20 years, working alongside hundreds of small business owners and policy makers across many disciplines in the UK, Ireland and Europe. A serial entrepreneur, business leadership is part of my DNA. I am also a shareholder in companies involved in property management, food production and business development.

Over the years I have been a board member on numerous boards across enterprise agencies, further education colleges, post-primary education and the Federation of Small Businesses.

As a business leader, management consultant, organisational training director and business mentor, I have worked on the front line of leadership and decision-making within business and with businesses for a long time. I am the founder of identity-led business growth and use this throughout the book. It brings together my many observations into my Executive Identity Model® in the hope that by sharing this with you I will enable you to be a better, more rounded leader in business. I hope to provide you with an unfiltered insight into some of the highs and lows of leading in business and by understanding your Executive Identity you are forearmed and equipped to deal with the successes and challenges ahead.

INTRODUCTION

For a very long time we have understood the notion that leading a business is first and foremost about following a fairly set structure. Entrepreneurs, business leaders, development organisations and advisors across the world operate on the basis that businesses start up and grow in a similar fashion. If we have a knowledge of what this is, then generally most of us should be able to lead a company or a department with at least some degree of success. This approach offers us an important way forward, and understanding the nuts and bolts of what a business needs to develop strategically and operationally is extremely important. Understanding how to read a set of accounts in business is like understanding that you need cheddar and bread in order to make cheese on toast!

Fortunately, there are any number of books and articles about how you can best develop your business and the measures you can take to reduce the level of risk along the way. These range from templates to help you write a business plan, to undertaking market research into your customers. As a leader, it is important you examine every aspect of this in detail and continue to develop your knowledge and understanding of the fundamentals of how a business needs to operate.

However, unlike other business leadership books, this book is unique. It focuses on a different aspect of leadership, suggesting that setting up, running and leading an effective business or department is about more than just function. This book will show you that as a business leader you are supported and constrained by the type of person you are: your attitudes, values, goals, personality, approach to risk and so on. More specifically, how you identify.

Regardless of your age, as an adult, young or older, you have been influenced by many events and people in your life. There has always been the ongoing sociological debate of whether or not we are a product of nature or nurture.[1] In other words, as adults, are we a product of the genes we are born with or the influences on us as we grow and mature? Generally, most experts today believe that both play a critical role in defining who we are.

So it is with business leadership. You have not got here in a vacuum but rather you are a product of many influences. When you take up a business leader's role you don't just park these influences outside the door and take on a brand new persona; quite the opposite – they come with you full steam ahead. When you take on a business leader's role, you bring with you significant baggage that may support or hinder your job. Through the years you will have identified with certain attitudes, ideas, motivations, preferences, reference groups and influences attached to your life and your upbringing. A prime example might have been your peer group at school. Which group did you mostly identify with? Was it the 'Cools', the 'Party Animals', the 'Studious', the 'Quiets' or the 'Rebels'? Or were you more individualistic, not really enjoying being part of any group?

This book draws on the Social Identity Theory, which originated in the discipline of psychology in 1979 (Tajfel and Turner),[2] and highlights that our perceptions of our social selves (e.g. motivations, self-evaluation, association with certain reference groups) are pivotal to our decision-making. This book centres around the theory that by linking with a certain Executive Identity you will inevitably make business decisions and lead your business based on 'your type'. After an initial exploration in Chapter 1 of each of the identities detailed in my model, I will build on them throughout the book to assist you to have a greater understanding of the way you lead. Each type brings with it an attached personal vision for your leadership that is important for you to understand from the outset. Consequently, I have created the Executive Identity Model® with eight leadership identities to define the characterisations of business executives.

This is a 'self-help' business leadership book and as such encourages the reader to examine areas for change. I use case studies, tips and ideas, and exercises throughout the book to encourage you towards making positive changes to support your business leadership. Although these can be linked to a section on a particular Executive Identity, they are relevant to a number of Executive Identities and I encourage you not to skip over, as reading the book in full will provide you with a much better insight.

An Introduction to the Executive Identity Model®

> 'Never forget what you are, for surely the world will not.
> Make it your strength. Then it can never be your weakness.'
> George R.R. Martin, *A Game of Thrones*

Key Chapter Points

- ✓ You are the core of your business.
- ✓ As a business leader you are in business to succeed.
- ✓ A key to effective business leadership is understanding your Executive Identity.
- ✓ The Executive Identity Model® provides a useful guide to assist you in understanding your leadership style.
- ✓ Each Executive Identity has associated business leadership characteristics.

So why are you so important? Well, the one true and consistent common denominator in any business is the person at the helm – YOU! THE LEADER. When you decide to go into business, or take up the directorship of an organisational department, that entity becomes a significant reflection of you. Sure, there will be other influences, many personalities, numerous opinions and umpteen people who believe they could do it better. However, when it comes to the chase, the business will reflect its leader. There is no getting away from it, first and foremost you are 'in business with yourself'.

Questions such as 'Who am I?', 'Why am I here?', 'What is my role?' are of fundamental concern to all of us. If we go back far enough, many of the Greek philosophers, including Plato and Aristotle, questioned the meaning of 'self'. Just like musicians or fashionistas see their art as an expression of themselves, starting and leading a business is often an expression of who we are. The expression is not just in what we decide to go into business to do, but also in how we operate that business. It is important to acknowledge that leadership is fundamentally a way to make a statement of who you are and it reflects what you are.

THE EXECUTIVE IDENTITY MODEL®

In working with thousands of business leaders over the years I have had plenty of time to reflect on the predominant business identities that exist. By examining these and identifying with their business leadership characterisations, the aim is to assist you in better understanding your decisions and style. Generally, you will have a predominant type in your thinking and circumstances, that will stand out and create long-term implications in the business decisions you will make now and in the future.

There is no right or wrong answer to your Executive Identity – just an honest answer. Like most things in life there can be hybrids, where you may see yourself in more than one identity; however, you will have a predominant one. There is also a possibility that you may shift types as your own career life cycle changes. It is important that you examine the following descriptions and choose your Executive Identity through your

Figure 1.1

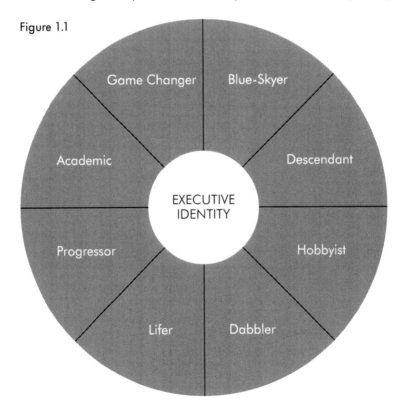

own self selection process at the end of this chapter. The rest of the book will assist you in understanding the implications of your choice. The eight Executive Identities are outlined in Figure 1.1.

THE EXECUTIVE IDENTITIES EXPLAINED

The Blue-Skyer

As the Blue-Skyer you are the typical creator and innovator such as the IT whiz kid, young artisan or inventor. You will recognise this identity as one of a business leader competent in your area of expertise, having worked with it, in it and developed an understanding of it over a number of years. You may well be young, still at college or recently graduated, in your 20s, with bounding energy and ideas, although not always. I have witnessed Blue-Skyers coming to business leadership after having had other careers and then giving in to a burning lifetime's desire to develop a product. So, it is most likely that as a business leader you have been immersed in your 'game' from a young age, often to the exclusion of all other interests. The thought of creating the next Microsoft, Dyson or Facebook has been just too compelling and has kept you focused for many years. You are all about creating a company that will enable you to pursue your self-interest, make money, create personal wealth and build a business.

Figure 1.2 outlines the six key characteristics of the Blue-Skyer. As a creator and innovator you can be very imaginative, especially with product development and design, but also with regard to business direction. As an innovator you tend to have a visionary understanding of what your product (or service) needs to achieve for your customer. You have an ability to see a problem and develop a solution to fill a gap in the marketplace. You tend to look where others don't and therefore find interesting ways to develop your product or promote your business. As a Blue-Skyer you are continually thinking outside the box and so your thinking is free and wide. You tend to view business success as two ends of a spectrum – boom or bust! Either way in your book it's worth a punt.

You are not frightened of hard work, being industrious and often working long hours, especially at the start when you are working on the commercialisation of your product. You are ambitious to see your product return results and succeed. You are comfortable with competition and will often compete

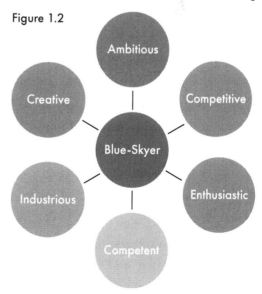

Figure 1.2

against time, your past performance and competitors. Ambition can be an underlying value that runs throughout your business leadership. In some ways your own personal success can be less important to you than the success of your product. Generally, you are interested in maintaining high ethical standards and it is important to keep this in check. Having ambition is a positive characteristic so long as it doesn't cross any ethical lines and harm others – either staff, customers or the community in which you operate.

When your business was starting out there was likely to be little personal commitment in your life and certainly limited financial burden other than finding the funds to have a good social life at the weekends. In most cases, you have very little to lose and lots to gain by pursuing your business interests. The most you could have to lose by going into business might be the need to start a more traditional career in a few years when some responsibilities kick in, or when you have accumulated start-up debt which you need to address. Perhaps also a little face among friends and family if things don't work out as expected.

As the Blue-Skyer you are genuinely enthusiastic for your product development and any new progress is a strong motivator for you. This can be catching and so you tend to bring others around you into your enthusiasm. You are also creative and therefore come up with interesting ways to show your enthusiasm to your team. You tend to like bringing interesting ideas into the team to allow others to express their enthusiasm, such as ringing a bell in the office when new targets have been achieved.

The Descendant

As the Descendant you are the next generation family member leading the business. When we look at countries and regions such as South America, China, India and Asia, whole economies thrive on the success of generational family businesses. The idea of a family business probably creates an image of a small car dealership where the son is cleaning the cars for sale while the father ponders on the day he will proudly sign over the shareholding. Yet some of the biggest players in global business started out as family businesses, including Ford and Walmart. Given that 69 per cent of family businesses in the world have members of the next generation working in the company, the Descendant is an important identity. To be clear, a family business is when (usually) the children take over the running of the business from the parents and subsequently maintain the income for the family. Hard-working in their approach, family businesses are a mainstay of our economy and most common in the agricultural, farming, fishing and construction communities.

Within the small and medium business community, there is probably no more dangerous a scenario than when a business is moving from one generation to the next. They do not have a good survival rate. Overall, less than 33 per cent of our businesses survive the move from first to second generation and only 50 per cent (so 15 per cent overall) of these survive from second to third generation. Although there will be some local variations in countries and regions the statistics are not good!

With that in mind, there is typically one of two scenarios that now occur in generational family businesses. In the first instance there is a keenness by the child to take on the reins of the company. You can be affirming to the previous generation that all their hard work has paid off and this is probably much more likely if the business is profitable and running successfully. From a very early age the Descendant has been exposed to the daily rhetoric around the parent's business. The evening dinner table has provided a ritual of updates on the operations of that day's business, ensuring that the future management of the company is at the very heart of the next generation's DNA. The Descendant is totally exposed to the micromanagement of the business and so accepting the role of the future running of the family business is the only career path that seems feasible.

There is, of course, the opposite scenario. The one where there is a great reluctance and resentment on the part of the Descendant to continue on the family tradition. Not surprisingly this is more likely when the family business is just 'ticking over' and maybe a little tired. It generates an average living standard for the family members but with a lot of challenges and issues. These can be economy, equipment, staff or all of the above. For this Descendant a different personal path would be much more appealing but they don't want to upset their parents. The children have watched the struggles of their parents and want no part of it, and yet there are family ties that are much stronger than business ties. There could also be a fairly stubborn parent in charge (as with many farming families) where an alternative career for the child is just not an option!

Figure 1.3 provides a summary of the six main characteristics of the Descendant. It is likely you have grown up eating, sleeping and breathing the family business, either consciously or unconsciously, and so you have a 'behind the scenes' understanding of how it operates. You may well have worked in the business in a part-time role when you were still at school, during the summer holidays or at weekends. As the business has been an integral part of your life for many years, both professionally and personally, your relationship with it tends to be personal and intuitive. Your knowledge and understanding of the business run deep and this intuition can assist you in making informed business decisions. You will have a lot to contribute to the group dynamic of the business and this is an important asset to use and assist the business to grow. Due to the longevity of the business there tends to be a culture of affirmation that you can adopt.

Figure 1.3

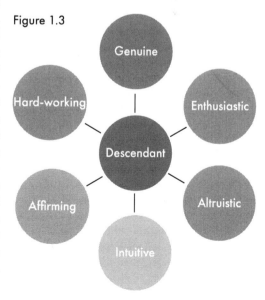

The culture is one where the staff is seen as a team rather than a group of people undertaking a task.

You are not a stranger to hard work and are likely to have seen your parents and other family members working long hours. This ethos is generally passed on to you and dedicating a lot of time to the family business comes as second nature. You are enthusiastic for the business to succeed as you have a vested interest in its long-term success. You appreciate that you have (or will have) significant, if not all, shareholding and therefore ownership in the business in the long term, and will have a genuine commitment to business success that is different to that of any employee. You tend to be altruistic and are willing to share the benefits of the business with your employees. Generally family businesses operate within communities and so your contribution to the success of your community can be an underlying and strong value within the business. The pride and unity that can exist in a family business is genuine and difficult to replicate in any other type of business leadership.

The Hobbyist

As the Hobbyist, you are the business leader with a wonderful hobby, creating (or selling on) something that friends and family really love. With the best possible intentions your friends and family engage with the mantra 'why don't you sell this?' And so a selling process emerges through perhaps country markets, online shops, retail outlets or house parties. This type of business is particularly prevalent within the food, clothing and craft sectors. The common denominator is that each Hobbyist believes that the business can become an entity that will give them an income and has the potential to grow.

There are usually fairly low barriers to getting started and the business is most likely to have evolved slowly over a period of time. Figure 1.4 provides a summary of the six key characteristics of the Hobbyist.

If you identify as a Hobbyist then you are probably, I believe, in one of the most difficult categories for business that exists! Fairly early on you had to decide if there were enough sales from your hobby to allow you to financially give up your job or make that capital investment you needed to buy more stock. If your life seemed like it had hit a mundane zone, then you are more likely to have taken the plunge and made

Figure 1.4

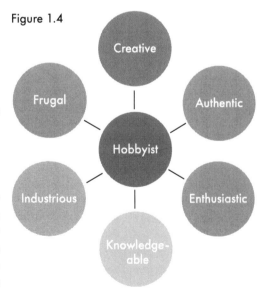

your hobby into a full-time business. You are possibly now having some selling success and so there is some evidence to suggest it could work. You have had to be frugal with your resources in order to get your business moving in the first place.

There are certainly many success stories of businesses that started out this way, including the White Company and Party Pieces, which was founded by the mother of the Duchess of Cambridge. Hobbyists make a significant contribution to our economy from Uber drivers, house sitters, cake decorators – to name but a few. Authenticity tends to be important to you as it underpins your craft and the story that is important to your consumers – handcrafted, handmade, local and so on.

You are highly enthusiastic and knowledgeable about your craft and your industry. If you are using a craft that you have learned or been handed on by the previous generation, then it is likely that your product reflects authenticity and originality in the marketplace. You are likely to have been a person in employment or at home looking for an option to increase your income. If you are making money at your hobby, then it has become a business. You tend to be industrious and work very hard having to undertake many of the business functions yourself as the business does not grow quickly enough to allow you to afford to employ others at a senior level.

The Dabbler

As the Dabbler you are pottering in business. You may have a full-time job or main business, while also having a small business, or investment in a small business, on the side – typical of some private landlords, business dragons or retail shop owners. Or you may have taken early retirement or left your job with a pay-out of some description. Dabblers usually have some excess funds from their career and want to have an extra income or are not quite old enough to retire. Generally, you are not really interested in a whole new career but rather a way to make your funds grow without too much input. The additional business also helps you to satisfy a yearning to be an entrepreneur without the risk of all your income coming from a business.

In the first instance, if you are a Dabbler who is also an investor, you have time to look around for a 'best fit' business for your skills and expertise so that you can maximise your input. As the Dabbler you tend to have a 'spare' stash of money that you are willing to put into a business to try to generate some additional income. This can be as a result of the fact that you work full-time on your 'main' career, or you have just had a tax break or a windfall from your retirement plan. Whatever the circumstance, you can afford a little risk with your resources and can take your time to look around for the most lucrative business idea.

Like the Blue-Skyers, for very different reasons, Dabblers believe they have little to lose as the funds they have tend to be excess. They are usually prepared to lose what they invest. Like the Hobbyists, you may wish to experiment in a sector where you have had a lifelong interest such as art, cars, coffee or cake-making. Strangely enough, Dabblers quite often take up opportunities in retail – maybe open a small shop or café – something that they believe will not be too demanding and help them to meet people daily. For those of you who run cafés and restaurants you will know the truth about what a demanding, low-margin business it can be. It is difficult to think of those who have made this type of business a success mainly because the goal is not to grow but rather pass time. I'm sure most of you can think of a few people in your community who have gone down this path.

You can normally take a longer-term approach to the development of your business and are prepared to wait for the returns. Given some of the difficulties we have discussed relating to short-termism, this attitude can be a real advantage for your business. This coupled with your career experience can make you an attractive investor for other Executive Identities. Figure 1.5 provides a summary of the six main characteristics of the Dabbler.

You are flexible in your approach and if you have ever watched any *Dragons' Den* programmes, this is exactly what the Dragons do – they invest in the businesses where they can have the greatest impact and make the biggest gains to propel their business and their investment forward. You could be an extremely valuable asset as an investor in other businesses as you could bring an insightful and balanced perspective.

If you have worked through a career already and have now decided to potter in business during your retirement, then you are likely to have worked in or led a team for many years. This will have enabled you to hone your communication skills and to ensure you are articulate when giving clear direction and support. You generally have less to prove than some of the other Executive Identities and can take a more helpful approach with staff. You tend to be more confident in your career and less threatened by others. As effective business leadership is no place to be timid, your confidence, gained through experience, can be your best friend.

Figure 1.5

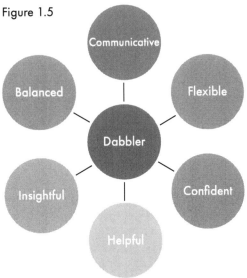

The Lifer

As the Lifer you have made a conscious decision that business is your chosen long-term career. You may not yet know what the eventual successful business is going to do or sell, but leading a business is what you want to do. Lifers can have a passion for business from a young age or can join the business leadership club a little later. As the Lifer you are driven by wanting to succeed in business regardless of what that business may produce or sell. If you come to the table later, in your 30s or 40s, there is generally a pattern of frustration in your career. By that I mean you are likely to have been 'caught' in a career path and to keep motivated you've moved jobs countless times before finally taking the plunge into business. The Lifer can be formally educated, or the training process can be a 'pick it up as you go along' approach. They can be skilled or unskilled. The common denominator is the need to be in business.

Lifers come in all shapes and sizes. They are quite often early adopters in that they take up a new product at the beginning before it's really got traction. They can be young Turks with many ideas and a lot of ambition. They tend to epitomise what we typically stereotype as 'true' entrepreneurs in that they start out buying or making something, anything, add on a few pence and sell it. It doesn't matter what the product is; what matters is that it makes money. There are many examples of success in this category, Sir Alan Sugar being one. Sir Alan is very proud of his struggle from rags to riches based on his own motivation, determination and pure tenacity.

As the Lifer you are most likely at some stage to develop a successful business, as you generally keep going until you succeed. You may already be there. However you have got here, or however long it has taken you, as the Lifer you will appreciate that business leadership has never been far from your thinking when you consider your career. Business is part of your make-up and it is unlikely that you can ignore this 'calling'. The product or service in which the business invests is secondary to the success of the business itself. Figure 1.6 provides a summary of the six key characteristics of the Lifer.

Not a business leader who gives up easily, you tend to have tenacity in bucket loads. In a consumer world where we are moving at such a fast pace, there are going to be many challenges in business leadership and the leaders who have the strength of character to stick to the agenda and overcome any temptation to give up are the ones who will inevitably succeed.

Figure 1.6

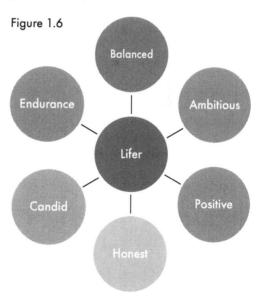

You have a high tolerance for endurance and an ability to persevere – even when things go wrong. Being a business leader means getting comfortable with ambiguity and enduring even though you won't have all the answers. You will have your wins and your losses but you have an ability to maintain your confidence. You have an inherent belief in yourself and your leadership ability that can enable you to see things through to the end and remain reasonably positive throughout.

You tend to be frank and honest in your leadership style, wanting to focus mostly on facts and figures rather than ifs and maybes, which tend to frustrate you. You prefer to take a balanced perspective on problems and therefore need your team to be open and honest with you. You tend to be seasoned in business leadership and, as such, candid. The key is to ensure that this doesn't move over the line to being rude.

The Progressor

As the Progressor you are most likely to be in business as a progression of your career. You have probably spent most of your career working in a company owned by someone else or in a large organisation. It is likely you were previously a deputy to your previous employer with significant managerial responsibilities. You are therefore going to know a significant amount about the industry in which you are operating and have the desire to be in business for yourself and 'do it for yourself'. There is a possibility that you have climbed the career ladder as far as you can go and yet wish to climb further, stepping out on your own seems the next natural career move. You may well have become frustrated with an incompetent boss (your thoughts) or financial waste such as over-staffing or over-buying.

As the Progressor you would have been the 'second-in-command' in your previous employment. In that role you are likely to have become very familiar with your industry. You will have worked your way through most aspects of delivering the service and you know and understand it well. As you have been working in the industry for many years, your move into your own business is probably smoother than some of the other Executive Identities. You probably have a good knowledge of the supply chain and you may, for example, be able to bring suppliers with you. You will have put a lot of thought into your new business and your ability to enter the market at a more advanced stage can be something you can maximise in your business leadership. This is a common business start-up within the service sector and in particular IT, hairdressing, beauty spas, recruitment and catering. Figure 1.7 provides a summary of the six main characteristics of the Progressor.

As a deputy you will most likely have a friendly approach to your staff, customers and suppliers, and this approach has served you well. You can bring this into your business leadership, except you also need to know when to be the boss rather than a friend. You can struggle with this at times, especially at the start of the business formation. You are courageous and have taken the step to move into business on your own,

Figure 1.7

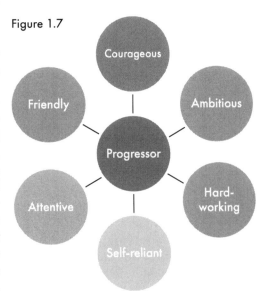

when you could have stayed in a role with less risk while still having responsibility. You are most likely therefore in business because you believe you could do it better on your own, or you could make more money on your own rather than as second-in-command in someone else's business.

You are ambitious to make your business succeed and will work hard to get it growing. You can be very self-reliant, knowing that this is an important opportunity for you to carve out a business leadership role – perhaps the only one you are likely to have.

The Academic

As the Academic you have most likely come to business through an educational route. This Executive Identity is on the increase as we see more start-ups coming out of places of learning. As the Academic you will have benefited from significant institutional support from the academic arena. You are leading what is often referred to as a 'spin-out company' that has emerged from some form of academic institution such as a college or university.

You are normally educated and articulate and likely to be a 'faculty member, staff member, or student who left to start a company or who started the company while still affiliated with the [institution]; and/or a technology or technology-based idea developed within the [institution].'[3] Traditionally you will have had significant support to commercialise your idea through mentoring support, provision of incubation space and funding.

As the Academic you will proportionally have had greater exposure to potential investors in your business than any other Executive Identity. This is an advantage you can certainly use to grow your business rapidly. Your exposure to a variety of business mentors will have provided you with the business knowledge to move your business forward with practical implementation. You will also have worked on and with your product for a long time and you will understand its functions and shortfalls intimately. Your knowledge of your product gives you a unique lead in the marketplace; however by sharing this understanding with your team and investors you will propel your business forward much quicker. Figure 1.8 provides a summary of the six main characteristics of the Academic.

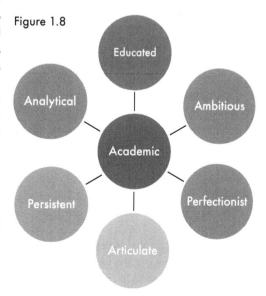

Figure 1.8

As a business leader focused on research and development, you strive for perfection, especially prior to the commercialisation of your product. You have spent a number of years perfecting your idea into a product or service and have a deep understanding of its functionality. You are ambitious for your product to succeed and as a spin-out business there is a high probability that you are very protective of your concept and reluctant to release the idea into the market. What if after all your hard work bringing an idea to life no-one wants it? There is a real possibility that coming to business from an academic perspective you are just not sure of your business acumen, as that element has not yet been tested in a practical manner. This can manifest itself in insecurity in your ability as a business leader.

You are naturally analytical in your business leadership, which can be a real recipe for success. Analytical business leaders tend to engage in fact-based decision-making based on proven data which can be the basis for effective leadership decisions.

The Game Changer

As the Game Changer you are in business to make a difference. Profitability and personal gains are overridden by the 'reason' dealt with by the business. If you are a Game Changer it is likely you are enthused by your ability to contribute to the community and value the support you receive from other community members. The community can mean the area in which you live, or it can mean the business community in which you operate, e.g. cosmetics, food manufacture or sportswear development, and it can be local, regional or global. As the Game Changer you are fundamentally in business to make a difference to your world whether that's your local community, the business community in which you operate, your region, your country or the world.

You are usually clear on your mission and that's to change the consumer's perception of an issue, either directly or indirectly, through the purchase of your product. There is a tendency to believe that these businesses will always operate as a social economy enterprise (such as Terracycle), but this is not always the case. There are many businesses run by Game Changers that are not social enterprises. One of the most famous in the 1980s was the Body Shop. The business leader, Anita Roddick, had a very simple plan to create a line of cosmetics that would rely on the consumer's concern for the environment rather than anything to do with vanity. By enabling customers to refill their bottles with cosmetics the Body Shop was cutting down on the use of plastics. Other examples include a business that is in food retailing and promotes the reduction of plastic packaging by asking customers to shop with their own storage containers. Or manufacturers of vegan flip flops like Chaco. Figure 1.9 provides a summary of the six key characteristics of the Game Changer.

You are unsatisfied with the status quo and examples of areas where you place your energy can include issues on the destruction of the environment, climate change, sustainability, Fair Trade, local sourcing or supporting local. It is likely you have put a lot of time into researching your issue to understand how your product can provide a solution in some aspect of a bigger problem. Whatever the definition, you see your business as an important catalyst for the development of your community and for you to achieve recognition from your peers. As a catalyst for change you bring tremendous creativity and energy to your business leadership. This enthusiasm will most likely be infectious and if others in your business share your vision your company can feel very alive and energetic.

As the Game Changer you are passionate about your 'reason' and you have made it your business to know your subject very well. As an altruistic business leader, you tend to be a team player and want all of your team to benefit from any success your business may achieve. You will entertain staff shareholding schemes and management buy-in options and ownership schemes. You are ambitious for business success more because it will get your 'cause' recognised than success for its own sake.

Figure 1.9

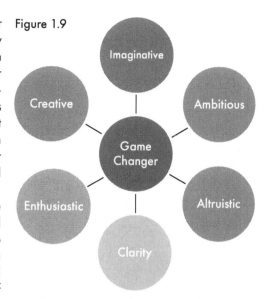

1. What is your main Executive Identity? To assist you, I have provided the following summary table outlining each Executive Identity and a summary of the common associated characteristics. Examine this summary and place yourself into your major identity.
2. **State Your Executive Identity** ....

Executive Identity	In Summary	Characteristics
Blue-Skyer	An inventor with many ideas and comfortable with risk. Not so interested in the detail and impatient for success. With the right idea and an ability to share you could be attractive to investors.	Ambitious Competitive Enthusiastic Competent Industrious Creative

Descendant	You are in business due to an accident of birth and loyalty to the family name. Business is part of your DNA for better or worse. Familiarising yourself with the formalities of business is important.	Genuine Enthusiastic Altruistic Intuitive Affirming Hard-working
Hobbyist	A craftsperson by trade, you enjoy the business you are in. You may not necessarily enjoy being 'in business'. As you are not too attractive to traditional finance houses you may have a longer lead into business than others and need broad shoulders to get through the start-up phase.	Communicative Flexible Confident Helpful Insightful Balanced
Dabbler	Usually you are joining the business leader fraternity after a career. Looking to invest a little time and money to gain returns, it is important you choose a product/service/route that you know something about and where you can use the skills you have. Be aware that very few businesses are part-time!	Genuine Enthusiastic Altruistic Intuitive Affirming Hard-working
Lifer	You have been born and bred with entrepreneurial blood. Perhaps circumstances have brought this part of you to the fore but however you have got here it cannot be ignored. Use your gut instincts but listen to others on the way and remember shares can go down as well as up!	Balanced Ambitious Positive Honest Candid Endurance
Progressor	You are knowledgeable in your field, often learning on the job. You often have a tenacity that you will need to succeed, and you can assist yourself and your business a lot by learning the key elements of operating a business.	Courageous Ambitious Hard-working Self-reliant Attentive Friendly
Academic	You have an academic idea to commercialise, often without that being your first route of choice. You are likely to have come into business by default and it's more about your idea than business being your chosen career path. Take plenty of business advice and don't allow yourself to get stuck in idea-development-idea. Commercialise.	Educated Ambitious Perfectionist Articulate Persistent Analytical

Game Changer	Passionate about your cause and with good support you can make a very successful business. Understand, however, that this may not be your goal. Seeing your 'statement' being made is enough satisfaction.	Imaginative Ambitious Altruistic Clarity Enthusiastic Creative

IN SUMMARY

As I highlighted at the beginning of the chapter, you will always have a predominant Executive Identity in your business leadership. However, I also briefly mentioned that your Executive Identity could alter as you work your way through your life career and this is an important point to remember.

Case in Point

It would not be unusual for a business leader to be working in a full-time job in a large organisation and being a Dabbler – pottering in a business venture such as a private landlord or running a retail store. This Dabbler may then leave their full-time position and become the Progressor, setting up their own business using their knowledge and expertise from their previous employment – maybe in design or IT support. This business could last for a number of years providing a lifestyle and then in retirement the person decides to develop their ice-cream-making hobby into a business to sell at local community functions and events.

The key is that you recognise your current, predominant Executive Identity as you work through this book. This will be very personal to you and very important in dictating every other decision you make in your business as it goes forward. Which of my identities do you fit into? Which one are you? There is no right or wrong answer. There are different objectives and goals. The most fundamental thing is that you are honest! Be honest with yourself. I am not being dramatic when I say that defining this category in the formative stage of business creation will have a significant impact on your business leadership decisions as well as some of your personal decisions for years to come. If you are already well-established in business then it may be your lifeline to helping you understand the decisions you make along the way – and why. The rest of this book looks at many important aspects in the formation and development of a business and examines the importance of these identities throughout.

Linking yourself to one of these Executive Identities is very important in understanding yourself as a business leader. This book explores your Executive Identity in detail and in doing so hopes to help you understand your actions and reactions in business leadership. Why you make the decisions you make; where you are coming from; and what is going to motivate you in business.

2

Your Executive Identity

'Play to your strengths.'
'I haven't got any,' said Harry, before he could stop himself.
'Excuse me,' growled Moody, 'you've got strengths
if I say you've got them. Think now. What are you best at?'
J.K. Rowling, *Harry Potter and the Goblet of Fire*

Key Chapter Points

✓ Your Executive Identity will have key strengths and weaknesses as well as opportunities and threats.
✓ By knowing your business leadership SWOT, you are able to build on your strengths and opportunities, and manage your weaknesses and threats.

There are strong and weak characteristics in any Executive Identity as well as opportunities to be worked with and threats to be managed. To illustrate this, I will use an adaptation of the S.W.O.T. (Strengths, Weaknesses, Opportunities, Threats) analysis grid – a simple but effective framework that can help in understanding your own business leadership. It first emerged in the 1960s from research undertaken at Stanford Research Institute to examine a business or organisation, and really gained momentum in business strategic thinking in the 1980s. I use it here as it also forms a useful tool for self-analysis in your own Executive Identity.

In using the model effectively there are some basic underlying assumptions that need to be followed in self-analysis:

16

✓ Strengths and weaknesses relate to your own characteristics, attributes and knowledge.
✓ Threats and opportunities are external to you as a business leader, often beyond your control, but within which you need to operate.

The key matrix that will be used to look at each Executive Identity is shown in Figure 2.1.

Figure 2.1	
STRENGTHS ✓ What does the Executive Identity do well? ✓ What advantages does the Executive Identity have? ✓ What is unique about the Executive Identity?	**WEAKNESSES** ✓ What hinders the business leadership of the Executive Identity? ✓ What needs improving? ✓ What are the skills and knowledge shortages?
OPPORTUNITIES ✓ What can the Executive Identity use to an advantage?	**THREATS** ✓ What are the threats to a particular Executive Identity?

THE BLUE-SKYER

Strengths and Weaknesses

You tend to be one of the main Executive Identities comfortable with risk, which really means that you understand that strategies can go in and out of popularity, and you have a flexibility in your attitude to deal with it. A little bit of 'so what?' in business is a good thing and this is something you are able to handle. This means that you can push the boundaries a little further and when you have small successes in your approach this builds your confidence to move forward a little further to assist you to:

✓ Develop a fast-growing company
✓ Respond to change
✓ Develop an approach that is attractive to investors, advisors and business development organisations

Although you are visionary in relation to product development this can hinder your ability to see the strategic picture for the business. Although your product detail is significant, your business direction may be only partially formed and this applies to whatever stage the business is at – start-up, growth or maturity. The issue is that you are now a business leader with responsibility for steering the ship and crew, and you have an important strategic role in the business that needs attention. Part of the issue could be an underlying lack of business leadership knowledge because you have come to the helm due to your passion for product development rather than a real thirst for business.

As an innovator you often prefer to work in isolation on product development and continually perfect the product. Therefore, your communication skills are not practised as much as they could be and you need to communicate your vision to others in your team so they can buy into what you can see and support the growth of your business. You can be impatient for quick business growth and often take a short-term view of reaching business success. It is vital to be aware that there needs to be a time when the product is actually ready for market and needs to be commercialised.

Opportunities and Threats

As a Blue-Skyer you can be very attractive in the business world! There is much greater support for this type of business today than, say, 20 years ago. You are likely to be exciting to investors and innovators. As you tend to focus on short-term returns and a fast-growing company, the Dragons' Den type of investor is an important player in helping your business to grow. This is even more important since this short-termism can mean that you are not as attractive to traditional sources of finance such as banks. Since you do have the opportunity to hit on a very successful product, coupled with the lack of traditional sources of finance, your business does need to get a high level of financial support through government grants and business support programmes.

Your requirement for significant resources for research and development far out-weighs many of the other Executive Identities. You are usually continuously working to stay ahead of the competition in a highly volatile marketplace. You need to be able to respond to the market and make changes quickly, and you have plenty of experience in doing so. Your R&D expenditure needs to remain proportional to the eventual product or service cost, to keep it competitively priced in the market. This is when you can maximise grant support.

Figure 2.2 shows a summary of the Blue-Skyer Executive Identity SWOT analysis.

Figure 2.2	
STRENGTHS	**WEAKNESSES**
✓ Visionary with product ✓ Confident ✓ Comfortable with risk	✓ Limited attention to strategy ✓ Often likes to work in isolation ✓ Impatient for success ✓ Lack of business experience ✓ Business ideas not fully formed
OPPORTUNITIES	**THREATS**
✓ Developing a fast-growing company ✓ Responsive to change ✓ A number of funding grants available ✓ Attractive to investors, advisors and business development organisations	✓ Securing finance for your ideas ✓ Continuous R&D by others ✓ Working in a rapidly changing environment

Case in Point

Five years ago, I was introduced to a wonderful young entrepreneur setting up a food business to produce a very innovative artisan product based on some traditional recipes. The individual truly knew their product and had undertaken a number of courses to perfect their production skills. They had a reasonable idea of their customer and market potential. However, their vision was for UK and EU domination within three years and given the product this was probably fairly ambitious. Like many businesses led by Blue-Skyers, the bank was luke-warm on any form of funding and the business needed cash. The projections were that the business would turn over €2 million in four years with very limited outgoings, again a little ambitious. The owner needed to raise €20,000 and went onto Crowdfunder. In the space of three months the owner raised the capital – by giving away 44 per cent of his business! Needless to say, the motivation two years later to slog it out for other people was not attractive and what could have been an attractive business closed its doors.

TIPS AND IDEAS

- ✓ It is important to improve on your business knowledge through programmes, mentoring, business advisors, networking and potential investors in the business.
- ✓ As a Blue-Skyer you should be aware that traditional banks are likely to view you as high risk and be a lot more cautious in any lending propositions. In some ways this leaves you more vulnerable as Blue Sky businesses generally need a lot of investment in the beginning.
- ✓ Even though you may be attractive to investors, don't get a swelled head – they know you are vulnerable and need their input.
- ✓ The best approach is to look beyond the money. What else can this person offer your business to help it succeed? Maybe they have excellent distribution channels, product expertise or market knowledge. This may be worth giving over a shareholding as it is always worth owning a proportion of something rather than all of nothing.
- ✓ You are likely to be a relatively impatient business leader – impatient with others not seeing your dream and impatient as to how soon the business should be providing returns. Like any other type of business leader, work on your patience as impatience can cost!
- ✓ An important consideration for you is bringing people with you – key stakeholders, investors and your team.

THE DESCENDANT

Strengths and Weaknesses

We have established that you are likely to have a knowledgeable understanding of the business and have a strong commitment to its success. However, as with most strengths we can usually find an associated weakness and so this particular situation means you may be too subjective as a business leader and need to familiarise yourself with the formalities of business to try to keep an objective perspective. If you are the Descendant who has come to the family business with no or limited external influences on your career, either through college or other work experience, then you are in danger of having limited business knowledge outside of the family perspective. It's a little like only hearing the opinion of your partner – it's not always a good thing! Whatever the circumstances or motivation, if you are the Descendant you are likely to have evolved into your role with a very mixed bag of knowledge and experience. The next generation often lacks the requisite skills and experience needed, and the parent owners who devote time and energy to developing their children before they join the family firm are in the minority.

Opportunities and Threats

The longevity is there for all to see and key stakeholders are confident in the stability that is created from one generation to the next in a family business. There is less fear of a business having a variety of people in senior management with constantly changing goal posts when there is a steady generational business. As the Descendant you have the opportunity to maximise on the story of the family business, including its long-term success, traditional influences and knowledge of your customer gathered over many years.

Family businesses tend to go through periods where they plateau and there can be a lack of innovation and investment in new leadership, equipment, premises and staff training. At these points the business can be under threat from those competitors who are investing and it needs strong business leadership to move forward and grow.

Figure 2.3 shows a summary of the Descendant Executive Identity SWOT analysis.

Figure 2.3	
STRENGTHS	**WEAKNESSES**
✓ You know your business well as it has been an integral part of your life for many years ✓ You've had significant 'on the job' learning ✓ You are heavily invested in making the business succeed	✓ Danger of being too subjective ✓ Lacking in 'professional' business knowledge ✓ Limited external input

OPPORTUNITIES	**THREATS**
✓ Promotion of the long establishment of the company ✓ Promote the family story ✓ Long-standing business relationships	✓ Needing to reinvest to keep up to date with newly established competitors ✓ Keeping your business competitive ✓ Keeping your leadership up to date and moving forward

Case in Point

I had the opportunity recently to work with a very successful (and sensible) generational construction company. The company had been run by three brothers for over 30 years. Each of the brothers had a life outside of the business, and two of the three had married and had families. Some of the family members wished to get involved and others didn't. Sensibly, each family member was empowered to make their own choice to either get involved or not as the case may be. However, if they did wish to get involved in the business, they needed to gain knowledge and expertise that was required and could be put to use. The owners wanted to continue to have control in the business, but they recognised things were changing and that the next generation needed to take the business forward. As part of the restructuring of the business, the decision was made that the owners would be the sole shareholders (for now) and the directors of the business would be made up of external expertise and family members all in paid positions. This was an ingenious solution that suited everyone and the business. There's always a solution!

TIPS AND IDEAS

✓ If you are a Descendant, then you need to come clean with yourself! Are you a willing participant, keen to become part of a long-term vision and work hard? If so then make sure you learn all you can on the job while the original leaders are around. Soak up your knowledge like a sponge and don't be scared to make your own mark.

✓ On the other hand, if you live each day resenting the people and circumstances that placed you in this position then I suggest you need professional business help. There are some fantastic experts around – perhaps your own accountant or solicitor? Whoever it is, I suggest some external review of the business that will provide you with some fresh thinking to either continue to learn and grow with the business, or to assist you with an exit strategy that works for everyone.

THE HOBBYIST

Strengths and Weakness

As the Hobbyist you have huge enthusiasm for your product. It has been your craft for some time and you tend to know it very well. You have been successful with some sales and you have now made your passion into your business. Your knowledge of your product is really what makes the business succeed. You tend to stay close to your customer throughout your business leadership as you are also active in the selling function and so you can respond quickly to feedback from your customers. One of the most difficult stages for you is taking the plunge into business in the first place and having the confidence that your hobby can create a living for you. After that initial jump you can tend to get a little focused on the micro development of your product production. Your overall business knowledge can be lacking outside of production and customer relations, which can stagnate the growth of the business. Growing a personal hobby into a full-time business is difficult. Getting financial backing in the start-up phase from traditional banking sources is almost impossible. The problem is – you are the business! It's only your talent, passion and commitment that can prove there is actually a stand-alone entity here. Banks don't really like that. If the business has been going a few years and you are able to take a decent salary for yourself and it is beginning to turn a profit, then the banks may consider lending for expansion if you present a decent business plan. You may be more likely to attract an investor in the post-start-up phase, but the same issues are generally a problem for them too. Hence why I say this is a difficult business to get past the first few hurdles. You're pretty much on your own with no real interest other than your passion and the continued loyalty of your customers.

Opportunities and Threats

Unlike many of the other Executive Identities, you have a real opportunity to turn your passion into a business that could grow with the right support and direction. You tend to have loyal customers if you look after them and therefore an opportunity to add to your product offering and expand through this channel. The issue with most businesses that emerge from a hobby is the low barriers for someone else to enter into your space. For example, buying some stock and selling it on is not really a high-risk business strategy. The lack of commitment from financers means that you have to grow the business through the cashflow that it generates which is always a challenge and fairly slow.

Figure 2.4 shows a summary of the Hobbyist Executive Identity SWOT analysis.

Figure 2.4	
STRENGTHS	**WEAKNESSES**
✓ Huge enthusiasm for the product ✓ You know your craft ✓ Trying out your idea has been successful on a small scale ✓ Your knowledge of your craft and your customer is fundamental to business success	✓ Possible lack of 'professional' business knowledge ✓ You are not very attractive to financers as the business is very personal ✓ You are the business and without you it would not exist
OPPORTUNITIES	**THREATS**
✓ To build a strong business ✓ To turn a passion into a living ✓ To expand your customer base through business development ✓ To add to the existing product or service offering	✓ Potentially low barriers to entry for competitors ✓ Lack of commitment from finance sources ✓ Securing long-term business sustainability ✓ Turning a hobby into real income generation

Case in Point

I had the joy of working with a small craft beer producer. The owner, like most craft beer producers, started out making a variety of beers for friends and family. After getting some positive feedback the owner went on to produce more and sold it at his local country markets and in a few independent pubs. Also working as a sales rep for a large company, the demands of the beer-making and selling started to mean a 18hr/7day a week commitment for the owner with no time for anything else. With the difficult decision on hand of what to do next, he and I worked together. My advice was to put aside the passion for beer-making and let's start looking at figures. It was important that he differentiated between the fact that his job was impinging on his hobby and the need for his business to reach some very real targets to ensure he could survive.

TIPS AND IDEAS

✓ At the end of the day a good rule of thumb is – if you want your business to give you roughly the same income as you currently get, then your projected sales need to show at least three times that income over the course of the first year.

You need this to stand still and this allows for some wriggle room and start-up capital costs. Bear in mind that's not giving you any increase from where you are at today.

✓ A €1,500 monthly take-home salary means your business needs to be able to generate €54,000 in year one to keep your lifestyle. If it's not doing this, then you either need to accept that your financial position is going to reduce, and your business will run at a loss, OR rethink your start-up position!

THE DABBLER

Strengths and Weaknesses

The most common denominator in the Dabbler Executive Identity is your attitude to risk. You have a tendency to become informed and therefore you take calculated risks. You have also lived with risk for many years and are comfortable with it. Being able to take time to decide on your business investment allows you to pick and choose the type of business you wish to start or invest in. However, as you are more of a free agent than some of the other Executive Identities you can get involved in business leadership where you have limited knowledge of the industry you are operating in. This can leave you dependent on the knowledge of others, which may not always be the most insightful. If you have come to business from a large organisational career, you may also lack the detailed business knowledge you need to deal with the strategic and operational direction of any business. It is also important to consider choosing a product/service/route that you know something about and where you can use the skills you have as few businesses are ever part-time!

Opportunities and Threats

If you are a Dabbler who is a business owner, your circumstances and approach will enable you to give time to the business to gain traction in the marketplace. Businesses that are under-resourced in experience, time or finance have much greater difficulties getting off the starting block than those that don't. You are likely to have significant networks and contacts where you can tap into their enthusiasm and support the growth of your business.

As a Dabbler you may lack the real drive to make a business succeed as it's not your only option to generate your own income. Or you make choices that are more about your life goals than the good of the business. You can tend to prefer low-risk strategies and that's not always conducive to business growth.

Figure 2.5 shows a summary of the Dabbler Executive Identity SWOT analysis.

Figure 2.5	
STRENGTHS ✓ Ability to take some risk with the finance invested in the business ✓ Time to look around for the 'right' business idea ✓ Experience to draw upon	**WEAKNESSES** ✓ Possible lack of industry knowledge ✓ Lack of detailed business knowledge ✓ Reliance on others' knowledge and expertise
OPPORTUNITIES ✓ Your ability to financially resource the business ✓ Using your significant networks and contacts ✓ Engaging the enthusiasm of others	**THREATS** ✓ Competitors may steal a march if you are not too bothered whether the business succeeds or not!

Case in Point

One of my relatives in this position approached me to examine a business plan for their new high-street bakery business. Not to throw cold water on their idea, I pulled together a one-page document outlining the rent, rates and capital requirements for such a venture. This on top of the need to become a knowledgeable employer and VAT administrator at the age of 65 years was enough to make them rethink that holiday apartment in Spain where they could enjoy some time with their grandchildren.

TIPS AND IDEAS

✓ If you are a Dabbler, then it might be worth considering investing in some bonds and thinking of some more relaxing ways to kill time in semi-retirement than starting a new business.

✓ If the desire is too burning to ignore, then why not consider becoming a business angel and investing in a few other start-ups that would value your life experience. There are now a number of organisations and networks in your local business community that you can approach. This way you get to have an input using your vast experience and you might make a little money on the way.

✓ Given that governments are very keen to encourage people to support new start-ups in this way, there can also be some very interesting tax incentives.

THE LIFER

Strengths and Weaknesses

Your knowledge and understanding of business, usually learned through practical experience, can serve you well in your leadership. Your tenacity to make your business successful is admirable and yet, as with many things, it can also be your weakness. You are one of the Executive Identities comfortable with risk and sometimes need to keep this in check. For example, you may continue indefinitely with working on a product design that is not contributing to the bottom line and, in reality, should have been axed from the portfolio some time ago. This can make you vulnerable in business leadership as you are not always tuned into the dangers that could lie ahead.

As you are fairly focused on business success you can forget to take others with you and may not take the time to involve others in your team in key decisions. As you are confident you may not always see the value of others' input and this can leave your senior managers demotivated and feeling unimportant.

Opportunities and Threats

As the Lifer you will strive for business success and should that not happen in the first attempt you have the strength to keep going until you do. Your business experience can make you and your ideas attractive to financers and investors; however if you have some history of previous debt in business (with another idea not working out so well) then you have a harder job to convince others to support your latest venture. You may also be in danger of having too many business ideas, which can mean a lack of focus in pursuing the eventual successful venture. If you have too many ideas within your business, then that can also lead to a lack of focus and spreading your finite resources too thinly.

Figure 2.6 shows a summary of the Lifer Executive Identity SWOT analysis.

Figure 2.6	
STRENGTHS	**WEAKNESSES**
✓ Business is your career ✓ High levels of tenacity and determination ✓ Comfortable with business risk ✓ Ultimately succeeding is highly important	✓ Knowing when to involve others ✓ Lack of appreciation of the input of others to your success ✓ Too much staying power
OPPORTUNITIES	**THREATS**
✓ Hitting on that successful idea ✓ Others could back your tenacity ✓ With the right idea you can be attractive to investors	✓ Too many business ideas so lacking focus ✓ Spreading finite resources too thinly

Case in Point

Working with Lifers can be very exciting as these businesses grow and grow because of the person at the helm. I have had the privilege of observing a true 'Lifer' over 30 years. The business owner started off selling frozen food out of her garage to the local community. After being approached by a number of local cafés and restaurants to supply, it was clear over time that there was a gap in the market for effective and efficient distribution of fresh and frozen foods to the hospitality sector. To undertake this work, the business needed to move to new premises, purchase vans and lorries, and create the momentum to grow the business. The last I heard the business is still operating with the original owner at the helm, and about to make a €6 million investment in a second warehouse extension and to create a significant number of jobs. The important point is it can be very successful – but you are in it for life!

TIPS AND IDEAS

✓ As a Lifer, you are reasonably comfortable with change and moving in different directions to ensure eventual business success.
✓ Knowing when to change direction, bail out or keep going is important.

THE PROGRESSOR

Strengths and Weaknesses

Working as a deputy in another business or as a player in a larger organisation, you will know the industry that you are now part of. You will have an understanding of the customers, suppliers and key players. The issue is that you may not have these detailed or long-term relationships in your own right but rather through your previous boss. This can make the relationship-building more difficult but not impossible. You just need to be ready for some rejections as there will be those who will be loyal to your previous employer. Although there is no doubt about your capability to do your job and deliver your product or service, the reality is you have never led your own business. There is a chance that your detailed understanding of the functions of running a successful business are lacking, and it is important that you familiarise yourself with the requirements to run a business profitably.

Opportunities and Threats

As you tend to know your industry well you are perfectly placed to identify gaps in the market and build your business on addressing those gaps. With your industry contacts and knowledge, you can also, to some extent, skim over the start-up phase of the business and jump quickly to the growth phase. Importantly, trying to grow a successful business out of undercutting your previous employer is not a long-term business strategy. If it's not already obvious then you need to have a lot more to your business offering to sustain it beyond the initial honeymoon period.

Figure 2.7 shows a summary of the Progressor Executive Identity SWOT analysis.

Figure 2.7	
STRENGTHS ✓ Sound knowledge of your industry ✓ An understanding of your customer ✓ Knowledge of the supply chain	**WEAKNESSES** ✓ Possible lack of business leadership knowledge ✓ Lacking in own business networks
OPPORTUNITIES ✓ Building a business that addresses gaps in the market ✓ Ability to enter the market at a more advanced stage with lower start-up costs	**THREATS** ✓ Price-cutting is not a long-term business strategy that can be sustained

Case in Point

From working with many restaurants I have realised that a significant number are borne from the Progressor. Many chefs have left their employment to set up on their own and there are many successful examples – including the famous Michel Roux. What I have also noticed is that most Progressors have learnt the hard way, through trial and error, and making mistakes along the way. It doesn't need to be like that and with all the business support programmes available it shouldn't be like that. Even the basic knowledge and understanding that these provide can help divert a crisis or at least save you a few headaches along the way.

TIPS AND IDEAS

✓ I have noticed an important trait in Progressors – an inherent desire to make the business succeed and a real tenacity in those who stick with it. Often working long hours, you can be rewarded with a decent lifestyle and in some cases greater flexibility to operate how you see fit than as a deputy in a job.

✓ It is crucial that you ensure you understand the running of the business element as much as the delivery of your service. Like Laurel and Hardy, it is impossible for one to perform successfully without the other. You should do this as early as possible after you have made a serious decision to go into business. In reality it should have been done before you left your previous employment.

THE ACADEMIC

Strengths and Weaknesses

As the Academic you will have a detailed theoretical knowledge of your product. You are likely to have been mentored well and have a detailed theoretical understanding of business. On the downside, a significant part of your career before business was in the academic world and so your practical business leadership knowledge may be limited. If you have ever parented a newborn baby for the first time you will understand that you can go to all the parenting classes you like but nothing much prepares you for such a life-changing event.

Opportunities and Threats

Coming from academia and wanting to commercialise your research means you most likely continue to have more exposure to potential investors for your business than any of the other Executive Identities. You have a real opportunity to involve investors, business dragons, venture capitalists and business angels in your business to propel it forward in a fast and efficient way, using their money and their knowledge. However, as you are commercialising research you can tend to dither and look for perfection before market entry with the new product or adaptations. This can cost the business dearly through the threat of other competitors securing the market share before you.

There are now numerous funding programmes to support this type of business and many emerging innovation departments within universities. I have worked with many small businesses that accessed government grant programmes to support the set-up and growth of a business. However, with university spin-out businesses the funding is usually significantly higher, longer lasting and further reaching. There is a valid reason for this as these businesses are emerging from a concept and quite often have many hoops to jump through to get a product or service commercialised.

As much as supporting innovation is to be welcomed and there are some very successful examples of this type of business, the 'over-funding' of this sector can cause a problem. As an Academic you need to understand the difference between having a viable, sustainable business and a business that is prolonged and propped up through grant funding and ongoing mentoring support. Like the Blue-Skyers there is an understanding that funding is required to move from your research idea to something that is commercially viable. However, the grey area created by grant funding, in particular, can cause a false sense of security. A dependency can be created that decreases the need to sell.

Figure 2.8 shows a summary of the Academic Executive Identity SWOT analysis.

Figure 2.8	
STRENGTHS	**WEAKNESSES**
✓ Sound knowledge of your product ✓ Several years perfecting your product ✓ Usually engaged with a number of business mentoring opportunities	✓ A possible lack of understanding of business leadership ✓ Theoretical knowledge vs practical implementation
OPPORTUNITIES	**THREATS**
✓ Significant institutional support ✓ Higher levels of exposure to potential investors ✓ High levels of grant funding support	✓ Ongoing competitive product development in the industry

Case in Point

I was delivering a training programme for small business start-ups to support the entrepreneurs to examine business growth strategies. One of the participants was an engineering graduate and during his Master's programme he examined the idea of a locking system for urban bikes. He was participating in my programme five years later without a sale and yet had accessed over €180k of funding. When we discussed the growth strategy for the business his focus was on how to access further funding to 'tweak' the product. Needless to say, the other entrepreneurs in the room were aghast and after spending some time trying (unsuccessfully) to change his direction to examining potential customers in retail, public sector, etc. we all gave up. Much like any future funding bodies I suspect.

TIPS AND IDEAS

✓ As an academic it is important that you work with business mentors throughout the commercialisation of your idea. Soak up advice like a sponge and act on the advice.

✓ Most importantly, you need to undertake regular checks on where the business is at. There is no specific rule as to how long you keep updating a product prior to market entry or how much funding an idea requires to get it to market.

✓ It is important to get feedback from potential customers at all stages to assess product desire and to support ongoing developments. Website landing pages, consumer focus groups and prototype testing are all important tools you can use on your journey.

✓ It is important that you see commercialisation as the core of business functionality.

THE GAME CHANGER

Strengths and Weaknesses

This category is also often associated with smaller artisan producers. It is believed by the consumer that these business leaders want to either preserve traditions within their community or promote a particular cause. It is important that you give yourself permission to grow your business and your leadership. In your quest to make a point through your product you should be mindful of developing a blinkered view. It is always a good idea to involve others who will give a wider business perspective on key strategic decisions. If you are at the start-up stage of your business, it is important that you objectively review if your passion can actually be turned into a successful business.

Opportunities and Threats

That said, many causes with good support can make very successful businesses. In fact in the current era consumers are more receptive to championing the right cause than ever before. We only have to look at the success of Greggs vegetarian sausage roll to see it in action. I believe it is one of their most successful products ever. However, sometimes your passions are not always shared by others, leading to frustration with some key stakeholders in your business. This is particularly relevant with financial institutions and potential investors, except for those who may understand your industry. You may find your choice for financial support is limited and much smaller than other Executive Identities.

When you are new to the market with a new concept, the cost of educating your consumer and supporters can become unproductive, and you should be mindful of having to spend endless resources on educating them. It is unlikely you will recuperate these costs if they become burdensome.

Figure 2.9 shows a summary of the Game Changer Executive Identity SWOT analysis.

Figure 2.9	
STRENGTHS ✓ Passionate about your game-changing cause ✓ Great knowledge about your subject	**WEAKNESSES** ✓ Passion overload ✓ Appreciating the business element of what you need to do ✓ Objectively reviewing if your passion is actually a business ✓ Impatience with others not understanding your issue
OPPORTUNITIES ✓ Strong businesses can be built on a game-changing idea ✓ Landscape is very positive for game-changing businesses	**THREATS** ✓ Key stakeholders may not understand your passion ✓ Needing to spend too much time and energy educating customers before a sale

Case in Point

I have worked with a number of Game Changers, particularly within the food and drinks sector. My biggest insight was when I worked with a café owner about 20 years ago. A vegetarian by choice, he located his business in a university student area to bring vegetarian food to young people at a time in their lives when they were exploring new experiences and pushing the boundaries. He had clearly thought about his customer and where he could succeed best, given that this was well before vegetarianism was even a spot on the page. He was passionate about making the café inviting and he would spend many hours at the food counter educating his customers on the ingredients in their dishes. After a shaky beginning, his business went on to thrive and provide a good lifestyle for him and his family, and he got to build a reputation based on changing his customers' perception. The business was never hugely profitable, but I suspect if the same business leader was doing the same thing today, he may well have a few franchises spotted across the country.

TIPS AND IDEAS

✓ If you are a Game Changer, then you can be driven by many different motives.
✓ It is very likely that authenticity in what you do is very important to you and the community in which you operate.

✓ As you need to get your message across through your business, it is important that you have good marketing skills. You are in business for PR as much as the product or service you are offering.

✓ There is a strong possibility that you desire the 'we' in your approach to business and will want to be part of a wider group rather than operating on your own.

SUMMARY EXERCISE

1. Based on your Executive Identity, develop your own SWOT analysis, including elements specific to your circumstances. Be sure to think of your strengths and weakness as specific to you while opportunities and threats are external to you but will impact on your business leadership.

STRENGTHS	WEAKNESSES
OPPORTUNITIES	**THREATS**

2. Once you've examined all four aspects of your SWOT analysis look for potential connections between the quadrants of your matrix. Assess if you can use some of your strengths to open up further opportunities. And, would even more opportunities become available by eliminating some of your weaknesses? Then complete the following action plan to develop your strengths and opportunities while managing your weaknesses and threats.

	Action Required	Date of Completion
Strengths		

Weaknesses		
Opportunities		
Threats		

IN SUMMARY

Each Executive Identity has a specific SWOT analysis based on the characteristics of the identity. Knowing your Executive Identity SWOT will assist you in understanding your business leadership better, enabling you to be better at what you need to do. Often a weakness can be changed into a strength and a threat into an opportunity. The key is to use your SWOT analysis to develop a personal strategy to progress your business leadership.

YOUR EXECUTIVE IDENTITY IN THE BUSINESS LIFE CYCLE

> 'Believe that a future shore is reachable from here.'
> 'Doubletake' by Seamus Heaney, 1990

KEY CHAPTER POINTS

✓ The importance of the business life cycle
✓ The stages of the business life cycle and your Executive Identity
✓ Your Executive Identity comfort zone in the business life cycle

One of the most remarkable characteristics of leading your own business is that it provides you with the freedom to pursue your own goals, dreams and desires, and that it is your creation. For many entrepreneurs it is just this that drives them into business, along with the desire for a certain sense of freedom to 'paddle their own canoe'. We are usually motivated by the thought of doing what we love while developing our career and maybe even building an empire along the way. We are of course always encouraged by those who have made such a success of it, such as Bill Gates, Mark Zuckerberg and Richard Branson.

Like those who have gone before you, I am sure your main goal is, without doubt, to develop a strong and successful business. No one I have ever met in all my years of working with business leaders is ever in business to fail. In the long run, the aim of any business leader is to create a strong, sustainable and profitable company that may also be a platform in developing your social standing within your community and the wider environment.

So how do you do this? I really believe there is no such thing as an overnight success in business – let's take James Dyson as an example. He produced over 5,000 failed prototypes of Dyson vacuum cleaners over 15 years before the first successful model was launched. The key lies in playing to the strengths of your Executive Identity at each juncture in the 'business life cycle'.

THE BUSINESS LIFE CYCLE – A REMINDER

We are all born and providing we survive to old age, we will become a child, a teen-ager, a young adult, an adult and then a senior. In other words, there is a sequence of development we will go through unless there are some exceptions to our health or circumstance. So it is in business leadership. There is a wide range of information dis-cussing the business life cycle and the 'stages' a developing business will pass through. I have no intention of regurgitating it here except to provide a gentle reminder. Figure 3.1 provides a summary of the business life cycle.

Figure 3.1: The Cycle of Business

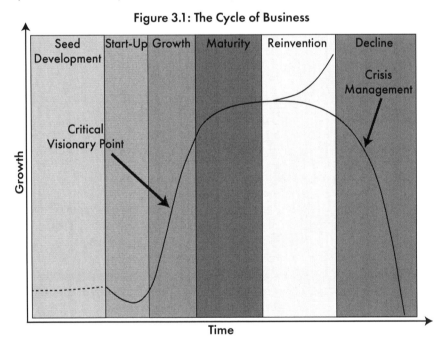

Key

Seed Development – when your business is just an idea

Start-Up – when you launch your idea and start a business

Growth – the business is generating a consistent revenue income

Maturity – when running the business seems routine

Reinvention – the business keeps going through innovation
Decline – the business reaches the end of its natural existence

What is important is that from the minute you decide to go into business, you're in the 'business life cycle'. This will see you journey from idea to start-up and, if successful, through to the growth and maturity phases. Like a vulnerable newborn, if a business survives beyond the start-up phase, it is likely to continue to work its way through the cycle in some shape or another.

How long a business spends at each stage depends on many factors, such as market changes, finance and personnel. Some generational businesses are still in their growth phase after 120 years, while other businesses are in decline after just three years. Some Executive Identities may even jump stages. Particularly for **Blue-Skyers**, they may have significant and fast growth after starting up and cash out with an early exit and their money made! Given the way our governments support small business start-ups and the high number of self-employed and non-VAT registered businesses, it is also clearly not expected that every business leader will grow a mature business that moves on to reinvention. Some Executive Identities may miss a stage as they are more likely to join the business life cycle later such as the **Descendant**. By doing so, this business leader may need to call on different leadership skills than those who are there from the seed development stage. I have summarised this in Figure 3.2.

Figure 3.2: The Executive Identity and Joining the Business Life Cycle

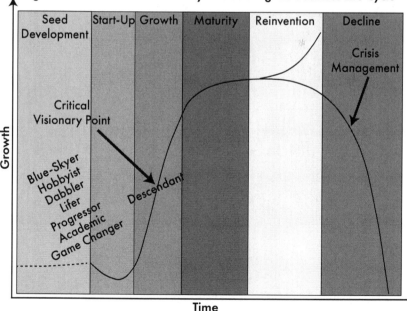

This is important as it will have a direct impact on the leadership approaches you need to consider when you 'hit the ground running'. I will now examine each of the stages of the business life cycle in turn and highlight where there are unique issues for each Executive Identity.

Seed Development

This is the first stage in the business life cycle and is the thought before the business is even in existence. You have an idea, but you haven't yet taken that crucial first step. This stage demands a lot of proof! Proving to yourself (and then to others) that you have an idea that can make a sustainable business. Now is also the time to do copious amounts of research on that idea. Research it in depth and across all aspects – financial, marketing and legal. Plan, plan again and measure what you are about to do before you do it.

TIPS AND IDEAS

✓ Talk to as many people as will listen to you about your idea – family, friends, business organisations, other business leaders.
✓ In the midst of talking to keen investors or friends encouraging you to make your ideas into a full-time career, make sure to talk to the naysayers too. Give them time and reflect on what they say and make an informed decision.
✓ The quiz in Figure 3.3 aims to assist you in thinking through your idea as the solution to a problem and to assess how your solution is better than others'.

Figure 3.3

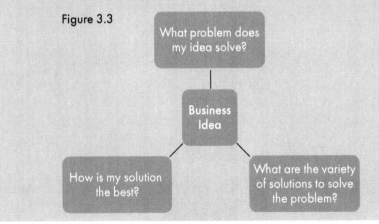

Case in Point

My memory of my chemistry teacher is vivid and long-lasting. She was a very practical person in so many ways and a true mentor for young people. During our practical experiment classes and just before we would start our new

> experiments, her words would ring out loud and clear and have remained with me throughout my career: Measure twice and cut once....What a phenomenal concept. Take stock. Think before you do. Once the substance is cut you can't go back. So, if you get the measuring part wrong you must continue with what you have cut!

However, the movement from seed to start-up is also about much more than the idea. In fact, if you speak to any bank manager about this, most will tell you that when they are approached for finance for a new business start-up their assessment to fund or not is 90 per cent about the person in front of them and 10 per cent about the idea. There are definitely key success factors (KSFs) for your Executive Identity (summarised in Figure 3.4) that you can draw on at this stage in the business life cycle (I have omitted the **Descendant** as you normally come to the cycle, at the earliest, in the growth stage).

Figure 3.4

Executive Identity	Key Success Factors
Blue-Skyer	Maintain your tenacity to move to start-up but ensure all research is done to prove demand.
Hobbyist	Market test that customer demand for your product can create a sustainable business.
Dabbler	With your wide networks there is an opportunity to bring co-investors and spread risk and skills base.
Progressor	Highlight the unique selling points (USPs) of your product that provide added value above your previous employment.
Academic	Ensure you research thoroughly the commercial viability of your product or service.
Lifer	Benchmark your idea against the industry and ensure this is the idea that can create a business.
Game Changer	Prove there is a sustainable business behind your passion.

The decision to go into business rather than have a steady income doing something else can be major (whether that's a steady job, investing your extra cash in the stock market, a high-flying career or staying at home while someone else is the income earner). We are also now seeing how many are feeling forced into self-employment as the only option to deal with the fallout of Covid-19, where it would not necessarily be their first choice.

Either way, the perceived shackles of employment (or unemployment) can be far outweighed by the new burdens and responsibilities demanded from a new and developing business. There is a total under-estimation of the fact that deciding to become a business leader, although no doubt very exciting, will affect you and those close to you for years to come. Like a marriage or any new relationship, the honeymoon can be short-lived, but the long-term impact will be with you permanently. Like any other life-changing decision, it needs to be taken seriously with your eyes wide open. Take all the time you need to think and plan not just the idea but about yourself – your goals and ambitions as well as your family. Think about their exposure in your new venture. Take your time and take it seriously. Once you're on the path the journey can be altered but not undone.

EXERCISE

1. Sit down in a quiet place, close your eyes and think of your vision of success. Write down a list of what success means to you. See yourself in that successful place as a result of your business leadership. Now put that to one side and think of going through a lengthy, rewarding and challenging process, only to end up with the same as or less than you have today. How well does that sit with you? Write down this reaction.
2. When you review this and you believe the journey is more important than the destination and you want to fulfil a personal need, then keep going!

Start-Up: New Business, Same Old Rules

Once you have fully thought through your idea and your own vision and are satisfied that you and the idea are ready to go, it's time to make it official and launch your start-up. If you have ever been involved in the birth of a new child (parent, uncle, aunt, godparent), you will understand that a newborn is extremely demanding as well as very rewarding. Grandparents will vouch for many tried and tested methods to deal with the everyday requirements of a new baby and yet sometimes the everyday issues can sometimes seem overwhelming. Just like starting out as a business leader.

It's exciting, extremely challenging, has many tried and tested methods to help you, and several new ideas and models that you can engage with. At the start a business's primary needs are the basic elements necessary for survival: the supplies and tools needed to deliver a product or service and a customer to deliver it to. Without either of these your business does not exist. It is normal to spend a significant amount of time adapting your products or services to respond to your customer feedback. What you need to know is that this is probably the riskiest phase of the business life cycle. Of all small businesses established in 2014:[4]

- 80 per cent made it to the second year (2015).
- 70 per cent made it to the third year (2016).

- 62 per cent made it to the fourth year (2017).
- 56 per cent made it to the fifth year (2018).

These numbers show that just over half of all start-ups survive to their fourth year. It will be no surprise that the business is also fully dependent on you, its leader and the person undertaking all of the functions at this point. So being an engaged and well-organised leader is very important. Your role at this stage can be summarised in Figure 3.5.

Figure 3.5: Role of the Business Leader

Develop the Vision

Format the Business Plan

Negotiate with Third Parties

Establish the Business

Given this dependence on you it is important you use every advantage you might have in getting your business up and running. In the start-up phase it is most likely that any investors, suppliers or funders will keep a tight rein on your terms. This is to be expected. It is also expected that you will be honest with your key stakeholders about the potential of the business. Now is not the time to get creative with business plans to try to get your start-up supported. Unfortunately, there are many business plans sitting on bank managers' shelves that tell a great story and outline some very optimistic businesses with wonderful progression and growth. The issue is they are sitting on shelves.

A diligent lender will see through the fog fairly quickly and apart from not getting your much-needed finances you will probably have soured the relationship due to your dishonesty. Bank managers aside, you need to be honest with yourself. You need a realistic business plan for your business that is dictated by you. A template is simply that – a structure to support your thinking but what goes into the content needs to come from you. If you want a business to fund your lifestyle rather than create world domination, that's OK. Many of our businesses in this country are run in this way.

At this time in the business you are an important player to this group as the business has no real history in itself, but you do. Key stakeholders will be looking at your knowledge, skills and ability as a business leader and so you need to be prepared. Your Executive Identity provides you with certain USPs that you can sell to your advantage at this start-up stage, outlined in Figure 3.6. (Again, I omit the **Descendant** as you normally come to the cycle in the next stage).

Figure 3.6: Executive Identity USPs at Start-Up

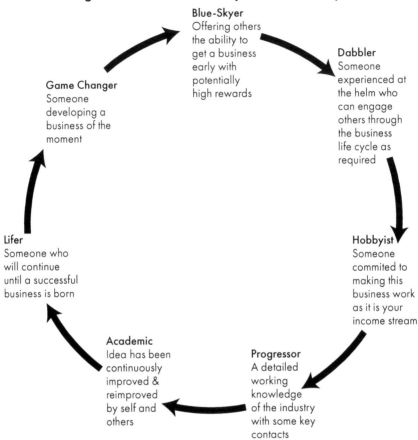

Blue-Skyer
Offering others the ability to get a business early with potentially high rewards

Dabbler
Someone experienced at the helm who can engage others through the business life cycle as required

Game Changer
Someone developing a business of the moment

Hobbyist
Someone commited to making this business work as it is your income stream

Lifer
Someone who will continue until a successful business is born

Academic
Idea has been continuously improved & reimproved by self and others

Progressor
A detailed working knowledge of the industry with some key contacts

EXERCISE

This is a busy stage in the business life cycle so managing your time must be your top priority to ensure that you do not become a 'busy fool', in other words someone who is always busy but not really achieving a lot. It is important to know how you may be wasting time in order to improve your time management. To make this assessment you need to keep a time journal. I suggest you keep this for one full working week and jot down your activities on an hourly basis. At the end of the week you need to go back over this and decide which activities are priority on a scale of 1 to 5 – 5 being the most important. I suggest that you then revisit any 2s and 1s to see where you can make improvements in the week ahead. It is important you repeat this on a regular basis and aim to reduce the 2s and 1s in your working week over a three-month timeframe. This discipline does work, and you will see big improvements in your time-wasting if you stick to this and do it correctly.

Growth

Once the company is through the start-up stage it will look to maintain its existence. At this stage the business should be generating a reasonable and consistent income. You should be taking a reasonable salary from the business and you should have the capacity to improve profitability and to employ others. This is a very busy stage. You are juggling a lot of different demands on your time and you need to use it wisely. It is important that you come into your own as a strong business leader at this stage and you also need to learn to let go to the wonderful people you have recruited and let them do their jobs.

The Saviour Scenario

At this stage I want to talk about something I call the Saviour Scenario. This is a position that I have observed in business leaders for a very long time. In this situation, the business leader maintains total control over most of the decisions in the business. There is little or no delegated authority to other members of the team, resulting in a complete bottleneck with the business owner. It is applicable to any business leader in any circumstance and is the fallout from the start-up stage in business development. It creeps up on you over time with no warning and can act as a death knell to most businesses. In many cases it is not a deliberate attempt to undermine anyone else, but rather a habit of having to do everything yourself at the early stages of business formation.

A Case in Point

Many years ago, I was visiting a business leader where the business was very much in the growth stage of development. The company serviced the construction sector and although worked on a contract basis they also serviced daily demands from their customers for immediate supply needs. I was warmly welcomed into the business and given a very pleasant cup of coffee. The business owner thought it best we meet in his office in case he needed to provide me with information during our meeting. I was merrily working my way through some basic questions to get an understanding of how the business operated when I got very distracted. I completely changed what I was doing. Although I continued to hold a conversation my focus was now on counting the number of times the business leader was interrupted at 10-minute intervals both by his staff coming into his office and by the transfer of calls to his phone. The common thread was that each person needed guidance on making their decisions and this ranged from the sales assistants on the shop floor to the finance director analysing the monthly management accounts. After 45 minutes I gave up and asked for a follow-up meeting within 14 days and that it needed to be off site.

When I pointed out the issue to the business owner, he stated that one of the issues he wanted to work through with me was his time management!

As my case highlights, the danger is not just to the business but also to you. If you continue in this space for any length of time with all the pressures such a scenario creates, then you are leaving yourself wide open to any number of negative health issues.

TIPS AND IDEAS

1. Make a start at delegating decisions. Start with small issues to improve your confidence in others and break old habits. This Delegation Grid in Figure 3.7 gives four key practical ways to help you be more successful with delegation.

Figure 3.7

It is also at this stage that the *Descendant* usually first enters the business. Given the description of the *Descendant* this is usually the earliest stage you might enter the business life cycle. It is not the easiest time to join a business with a leadership function and you normally have to 'hit the ground running'. Things may seem a little foggy at times but be reassured the mist will clear as you gain confidence in what you are doing.

Maturity

At this stage in the business life cycle running the business seems to become almost routine. Key staff members are carrying out their functions and the business has a firm hold within the industry. Revenue generation and cash flow are positive and consistent. The issue at this point, as the business life cycle shows, is not to sit back and admire the view. At this stage if you are not leading the business forward then, by definition, it will be going in the opposite direction.

The decision is whether you want to further expand the business, or you want to exit at this stage. If you decide to expand then the key is to ensure you expand in a measured, calculated and researched way. Having a successful business behind you is no guarantee of future success. It is, however, confirmation that you have dealt with many challenges, survived and have an idea of the things to avoid in the future. Many business leaders do opt out at this stage. It can be a time when you have had enough, and you no longer have the energy to 'start again'. It is important that you take real stock at this stage and decide first and foremost what you want.

Case in Point

Not long ago I was working on an investment plan with a well-established family business. The daughter had just come into the business with no particular practical skills to offer but with a university degree in Business. The mother had started a vegan café four years previously with the idea that she could have something concrete for her daughter to develop after university. The café had done extremely well and both mother and daughter were looking at investors to expand the brand. On the surface this all seemed logical until we started to look at the number of additional outlets they expected to set up within a three-year period. No fewer than fifty! Expanding from one to fifty in thirty-six months and with just two key players! We eventually secured finance for three additional outlets over three years and that turned out to be a comfortable timeframe for everyone.

Reinvention

The key to leading a successful business is to know when it needs to change. This stage in the business life cycle can be difficult for some of the Executive Identities more than others. For the *Lifer* the idea of starting over again can seem overwhelming and so exiting at this stage could be a good option. Or the first generation in the family business who may resist too many new ideas, which in turn creates tension with the *Descendant* who wants to action reinvention and innovation for the long-term sustainability of the business. If you are a *Dabbler*, however, you may relish the opportunity to go back for a second bite at the cherry of success.

Much like the start-up phase in the business, this stage involves extensive energy, new thinking, committed resources, possibly new skills and ensuring a 'best fit' approach to the overall growth of the business. Again, the focus needs to be on how the innovation will address a problem in the marketplace that provides enough of a customer base for all the additional effort. On the plus side, as the business leader you will bring a lot of positive experience and previous success to this stage. Probably the company that has been most successful at this stage of the business life cycle is Apple, when it changed its direction from computers to handheld devices in the early 2000s.

Decline

As a business leader, how do you know when your company is in decline? The most telling sign is when revenues start to flatline, i.e. revenues that grow less than inflation. The business may also have too many debts and is getting into difficulty servicing these debts. Although a business moving into this stage could be down to your negligent leadership, the downturn of the wider industry can be the real cause of this negativity. We do not have to look very far to see a massive industry in decline in our high-street retail. Some of the longest-standing, most experienced retailers of our time are closing their doors having been superseded by online shopping websites. Those that reinvented into online shopping will survive and grow, and those that didn't, won't!

Whatever the cause is probably irrelevant at this stage; the priority is to take immediate action to exit the business and minimise any collateral damage in the process.

YOUR EXECUTIVE IDENTITY COMFORT ZONES

Every business starts out small. Some, however, grow into global brands while some don't get past the start-up phase. One of the most important aspects of the business life cycle and your Executive Identity is that you are going to have stages in the cycle where you are most comfortable. The positive element of this is the fact that you are likely to perform your most effectively in this stage. You are most likely to thrive in this stage and really implement all that's positive about your business leadership skills. The downside is, as with human nature, we like our comfort zones and so it is very easy

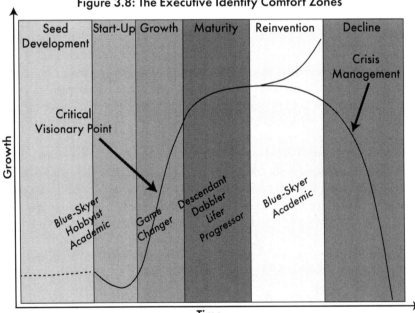

Figure 3.8: The Executive Identity Comfort Zones

for you to get stuck! Figure 3.8 shows your most comfortable zones in relation to your Executive Identity.

How to Avoid Getting Too Comfortable in Your Zone

The Blue-Skyer

As an innovator, the seed development and start-up stage is where you are most comfortable in the business life cycle. By its very definition, an innovator is someone who invents something new that doesn't already exist. This business would not exist without you and your ideas. As an inventor you can then come back on the scene again at the reinvention stage. The issue with inventors is their focus on the invention for invention's sake and it is a trap I have seen often and one you should be aware of. Like most things in life there is no perfect solution and therefore you need to move to commercialisation and then growth at some stage. The key is to undertake continuous pre-market testing and as the results change from negative to positive move on to the product launch.

Having examined your strengths and weaknesses in the previous chapter, there are certain precautions you should take to strengthen your business leadership. This could include putting a strong team around you to compensate for some of your management weaknesses. When you believe the business is ready for the growth phase you need to ensure you put energy into recruiting a strong team that will strengthen your business leadership functions. Options to consider include people with expertise in finance, marketing, production and communications.

TIPS AND IDEAS

1. In answering the following series of questions, you can have an insight into the best time to consider recruiting additional staff – a management skills check if you like.
   a. As the business leader how do you propose to manage the work involved in the growth phase?
   b. How relevant is the existing management structure in moving to growth?
   c. Is there a need for any additional management resource?
2. If you need additional resources, you are likely to require the expertise of a recruitment manager to assist you to build this team and you should consider working closely with one you can get along with.
3. It is a good idea to consider bringing another shareholder into the business. Not another inventor but rather this should be a businessperson with skills in bringing your business through the growth phase and to success.

The Descendant

The maturity stage is an important comfort zone for you as it is the time of business development at which you are most likely to join the business and the stage of the business life cycle that you know most about. Why? There is a strong possibility that you have heard all about the start-up and growth of the business at home, but it is unlikely the older generation will involve you until there is some level of stability in the business – at the sustainability stage. A key aspect of generational businesses is that they are only generational when the first business leaders believe there is something to hand on. Most family businesses exist into the next generation because the families are close and people care about one another. It is unlikely that a Descendant will be asked to join a failing family business or if they are it's because the current leaders believe it can be salvaged by the skills and expertise of the Descendant.

A key challenge for you is that you are joining the business at a time when norms and culture are already rooted in the very fabric of the business. As the 'new kid on the block' others will be nervous about the change you may bring to their 'family' and in many ways the family business is an extension of the culture and norms in your own family. This is a time of genuine concern for you and the rest of the team members as you both charter new waters and change. This can be compounded if the business is going through a difficult time and heading towards a decline and you need to undertake some reinvention fairly quickly.

The most successful transitions that I have noted for Descendants into the family business is when they know when to sit back and observe, and know the right time to step in and make their mark. You will need to make changes – even just normal business development requires change and you are the new business leader or 'business leader in waiting' so you will instigate change. It is crucial that you spend time getting to know all the levels of the business and understanding the team culture. You need to know the best and most undisruptive way to bring about change for the good of the business.

TIPS AND IDEAS

1. There are three key layers you need to work and understand as a *Descendant* in the sustainability stage of the business:

Layer	Activity
Front Line	Get to really understand what happens in this layer of the business. Spend time working on the front line. Learn to deal with these issues first-hand and lead from this position
Operational	Understand how day-to-day tasks get done. Observe how the team members work together (or not!)
Strategic	Be part of the long-term planning for the future from the start. However small, make your contribution from day one and follow through.

EXERCISE

By completing the following questionnaire, you will have an insight into the obstacles holding you back in your business leadership.

Question	Ranking: 1 = not at all; 10 = absolutely
How concerned are you about your business not being a success?	
How comfortable are you with change?	
Are those who say 'it can't be done' important to you?	
Are you aware of the external pressures that currently impact on your business?	
Do you take time out annually to update your business skills and knowledge?	
Do you network with other businesses at least once per month?	
Do you devote time to the strategic development of your business?	
Do you have a 'significant other' businessperson to act as your sounding board?	
Do you trust your staff to do their job efficiently and effectively?	

Where you score 5 or less you need to consider the measures you must take to minimise their impact on your business leadership.

The Hobbyist

It is likely that moving your business from an idea to start-up has been a slow burn. You are probably exhausted from making many personal decisions about your career and making your passion into a business. Given the demands of this process, you may not be fully focused on the business functions you need to consider and put in place to move the business to the growth phase. You can over-focus on the production of your product and the needs of your customer to the detriment of moving the business to the next stage.

Of all the Executive Identities you have to be the most self-reliant. The lack of financial and investor interest at start-up means you are more likely to need to fund any growth of the business through your own investment from savings or family lending, or from just the cash flow of the business. This can mean the budget for any growth activities like marketing, increasing production capacity, etc. can be very limited, making the move to the growth phase slow and difficult.

You are also relying heavily on your own business leadership skills which may be limited given that you have come to the business with an interest in your product rather than any particular business expertise or knowledge.

TIPS AND IDEAS

1. In the first instance, ensure you attend a comprehensive Business Start Programme. There are likely to be many run in your local area and you can find out more from your local government authority.
2. It is important to develop a one-year leadership skills development plan for yourself. To get this started please complete this short questionnaire to assist you in identifying the skills you need to develop.

   On a scale of 1–5 (5 being most knowledgeable), please rate your understanding of these key business leadership indicators.

Key Business Leadership Indicator	Rating 1–5
Profitability	
Financial management	
Developing a marketing plan	
Promotional tools	
Checking customer satisfaction	
Gathering information on the needs of clients	
Knowledge of competitors	
Developing supplier relationships	
Knowledge of pricing effectively	
Recruiting staff	
Staff training and development	
Operational management	
Quality systems and control	
Stock control	
Environmental policies	
Health and safety policies	

3. Using the results from the questionnaire I would suggest any indicator to which you award a 3 or below needs immediate attention within the first year. Note these indicators in the following grid and then complete the grid to give you the basis of a personal leadership skills development plan. You can then build on

this plan as you move forward in the business. It is also important to prioritise 1s and 2s.

Indicator for Development	Ranking Given	Person or Organisation to Assist	Completion Date

The Dabbler

When you examine the characteristics of the Dabbler in Chapter 1, it is not surprising that the maturity stage is your main comfort zone. As a (part-time) business owner or an investor you are really interested in making some additional income to an already steady income stream. Quite often your drive for success is about a comfortable life-style rather than the development of a big global brand. This is not to detract from the idea that a Dabbler is certainly interested in hitting on that high growth business for self and financial recognition – but not with a high-risk strategy.

You are at a stage in your career when you don't really want to take those big risks with your money, health or resources. You are only looking for some additional benefits to what you already own. In this respect, you may have a conflict between your needs and the needs of the business. Your leadership decisions might actually be counter-productive to the best interests of the business itself and more focused on self-interest. Although this will keep a strong hold over the decisions in the business and hopefully prevent any recklessness, the downside is the fact that you may hold the business back when it might otherwise have been successful through reinvention and your investment in reinvention.

If your personal needs are overshadowing the need for the business to reinvent and grow, then perhaps you need to consider your future role in the leadership of the business and even develop an exit strategy. Throughout my years of working with business leaders I have supported a number of Dabblers to undertake an option analysis to assist in choosing the best approach for them in looking to move the business forward. This would be a good exercise for you to undertake at this juncture.

EXERCISE

Work through the process in Figure 3.9 to assist your thinking and your leadership decisions at this time.

Figure 3.9

Step 1	Step 2	Step 3	Step 4
• Describe your leadership in the business as it is now in relation to frontline, operational and strategic input	• Outline the minimal input that you would need to undertake to move the business from maturity	• Outline the ultimate input required from you to enthusiastically move the business to the reinvention stage	• Note your preferred input option

If your preferred option outlined in Step 4 is *not* the option set out in Step 3, i.e. to enthusiastically move the business to the reinvention stage, then you need to examine your long-term business leadership role.

The Lifer

As the Lifer you are going to be most comfortable in the maturity stage of the business life cycle. Of all the Executive Identities, when you think of business success you consider a business with a recognised brand, employing a team of staff and making decent profits to be the ultimate prize in business leadership. It is at the maturity stage that you are most likely to have carved out a decent lifestyle for you and your family. You have surpassed the hard work and long hours often required at the growth stage and now have a team around you that can take some of the burden from your daily tasks.

Your role is now more strategic and so it needs to be. This does mean that you cannot sit back for too long and it is important that you are alert to the tipping point for the business within this phase. There is a very fine line between moving to decline and needing to reinvent. You need to be alert to the needs of the business and listen to those in your team and be open to reinvention either by you or by another business leader. Be aware that you have been a business leader all your life and you may believe that you know best. You may be reluctant to think about another 'start' (i.e the reinvention). Be open to the idea that you may not be the business leader who takes the company to the reinvention stage – that may be for someone else with more energy and vision. Whatever the circumstance, as a Lifer, you need to stay alert to becoming too comfortable in the maturity stage and be prepared to take action to reinvent the business, product or service when circumstances demand it.

TIPS AND IDEAS

1. The following table asks you some pertinent questions around your business leadership at this stage. In answering the questions, it is important to state if the timeframe is Red, Amber or Green

RED > 1 year

AMBER < 1 year

GREEN < 1 year

Warning Signs	Colour
When was the last time you approved the purchase of new equipment, machinery or software in the business?	
When was the last time you attended an industry trade show?	
When did you last examine the strategic direction of the business?	
When was the last time you attended a personal development event – workshop, training, etc.?	
When was the last time you were in your business more than 40 hours in the week?	
When was the last time you gave serious consideration to a new product or service development?	

With lots of GREEN answers you are most likely totally on your game and very much an active business leader with plenty of enthusiasm and motivation still to give. As business is in your DNA there is a reasonable chance you are still totally engaged.

With any AMBER answers then it is time to consider your personal and business goals. You need to consider what you want and whether you are still the best person to lead your business forward. If the idea of reinvention fills you with some degree of dread, then it may be time to consider your exit before the business suffers due to your lack of leadership consideration. With RED answers you need to take emergency action to stop business decline.

The Progressor

One of the main objectives of the Progressor in business is to create a lifestyle. The leadership challenge for the Progressor can be almost over when the growth stage is complete and you have entered the maturity stage. If we consider the reasons you went into business in the first place, it really revolves around a belief of being able to 'do it better', creating a better lifestyle for yourself and not having a boss. It is no surprise, therefore, that you could get stuck in the maturity stage, and without revisiting your leadership qualities and looking at reinvention your business is at high risk of decline.

There are many examples where the Progressor has operated a business for a number of years and then simply closed its door. Just consider your local hairdresser or café owner who originally set out on their own from previous employment. The business has fulfilled its function in creating an income and that has now finished.

So how do you know if your leadership is getting stuck in the maturity stage and what can you do about it? Being stuck is a little like treading water. You keep moving to stay afloat, but you are not actually moving anywhere. This is crucial to stop you drowning while you wait to be rescued but you are not actually moving towards shore. There are a number of key signals you should be alerted to around getting stuck as outlined in Figure 3.10.

Figure 3.10

Financially comfortable

Business revenues have been static for two years running

Your working days have become predicatable

Fear of risking the status quo

TIPS AND IDEAS

1. Figure 3.11 provides some suggestions to improve your outlook and assist you in becoming unstuck.

Figure 3.11

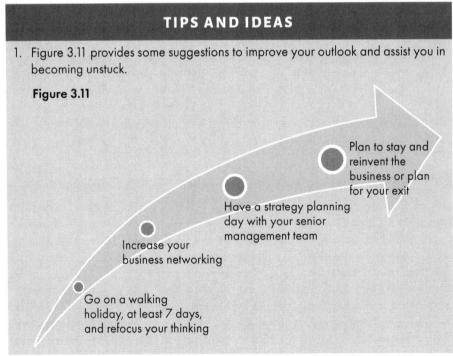

Plan to stay and reinvent the business or plan for your exit

Have a strategy planning day with your senior management team

Increase your business networking

Go on a walking holiday, at least 7 days, and refocus your thinking

The Academic

You will note from Chapter 1 that your biggest issue is moving beyond research and development to commercialising your idea. For this reason, you like the seed and start-up stages of the business life cycle. You then come back to this again at the reinvention phase. The nature of your Executive Identity is that you are most comfortable in an academic world where customers do not intrude. I want to reassure you that the most likely reason that you get stuck in this stage is a lack of business confidence and a lack of belief that your idea might actually work in the marketplace. Up to this point the chances are that your main support and advisors working towards commercialisation have also come from the academic world. This is not always the best mix to assist you in propelling your business forward. Getting some objective thinking into your business leadership outside of the academic world is healthy. A constructive non-academic business mentor will enable you to work through your fears and build confidence to strategically move your business forward. To make this a fully functioning business you will also likely need to focus on testing your idea in the marketplace. There are a number of tried and tested early industry exposure tools you can use, including customer feedback, review panels, focus groups and website landing pages, to name but a few.

TIPS AND IDEAS

The following table lists a number of key entrepreneurial traits. Assess yourself against them, giving a rating of 1 if your self-belief is low or 5 if your belief in yourself is excellent.

Entrepreneurial Trait	Rating 1–5
Self-confidence – a self-belief and passion about your product or service – your enthusiasm is needed to win people over to your ideas	
Self-determination – a belief that the outcome of events is down to your own actions, rather than based on external factors or other people's actions	
Being a self-starter – the ability to take the initiative, work independently and to develop your ideas	
Judgement – the ability to be open-minded when listening to other people's advice, while bearing in mind your objectives for the business	
Perseverance – the ability to continue despite setbacks, financial insecurity and exposure to risk	
Initiative – the ability to be resourceful and proactive, rather than adopting a passive 'wait and see' approach	

It is important that you are reaching 4s and 5s in all categories to have the confidence required for this road. If this is not the case, then it is important that you work on the areas where you see weaknesses as much as working on your business idea.

The Game Changer

As the Game Changer, the growth stage tends to be where you are most comfortable. It is your comfort zone because it is a very busy stage for any business leader in the business life cycle. It is the time when the business is stretching and developing. New customers are buying your products, new staff members are required to meet an increasing demand and your brand is starting to gain traction. You are also personally a very busy business leader. You are looking after the day-to-day business as well as thinking about the strategic direction. You are looking for additional staff, prospecting new customers and getting your message out there. Given that your Executive Identity is all about making a difference it is easy, however, to confuse a busy growth phase with business success. There is no doubt the reach of the business is increasing so it is easy to believe the business is operating at its peak and that your job is done.

As a business leader it is important to understand that the business still has room for further growth into the maturity stage. It is important to recognise some of the tell-tale signs that you may get stuck in this stage

✓ Just not enough work hours in any day
✓ Missing meetings with your staff due to workload
✓ Content with the way your business is promoting your message
✓ Not getting to business network meetings or trade shows
✓ Limited time to listen to staff

As the business leader it is important you take some key steps to move the business on to the maturity stage where you really start to see the fruits of your labour.

TIPS AND IDEAS

The flowchart in Figure 3.12 aims to give you immediate steps that you can take to push your leadership forward.

Figure 3.12

| Revisit the skills of your staff and delegate tasks with shared responsbility for results | Become a teacher, training others in the culture of your business | Increase your marketing budget by 5% to attract new customers | Provide upgraded service or product development for your existing customers | Take 3 hours in the fortnight for business networking |

BE COMFORTABLE WITH CHANGE – THE KEY TO BECOMING UNSTUCK

Figure 3.13

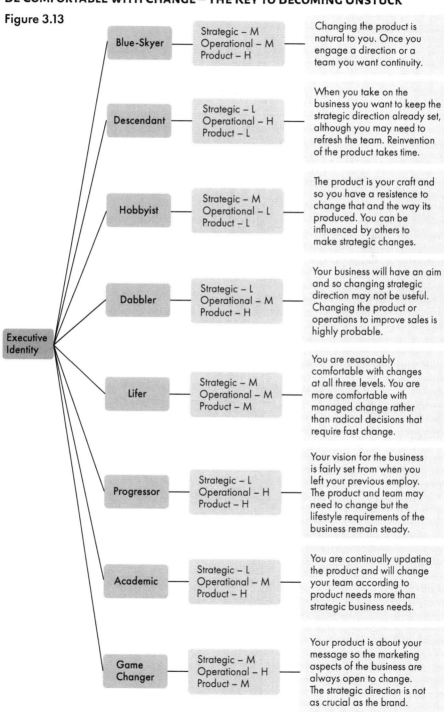

Blue-Skyer
Strategic – M
Operational – M
Product – H

Changing the product is natural to you. Once you engage a direction or a team you want continuity.

Descendant
Strategic – L
Operational – H
Product – L

When you take on the business you want to keep the strategic direction already set, although you may need to refresh the team. Reinvention of the product takes time.

Hobbyist
Strategic – M
Operational – L
Product – L

The product is your craft and so you have a resistance to change that and the way its produced. You can be influenced by others to make strategic changes.

Dabbler
Strategic – L
Operational – M
Product – H

Your business will have an aim and so changing strategic direction may not be useful. Changing the product or operations to improve sales is highly probable.

Lifer
Strategic – M
Operational – M
Product – M

You are reasonably comfortable with changes at all three levels. You are more comfortable with managed change rather than radical decisions that require fast change.

Progressor
Strategic – L
Operational – H
Product – H

Your vision for the business is fairly set from when you left your previous employ. The product and team may need to change but the lifestyle requirements of the business remain steady.

Academic
Strategic – L
Operational – M
Product – H

You are continually updating the product and will change your team according to product needs more than strategic business needs.

Game Changer
Strategic – M
Operational – H
Product – M

Your product is about your message so the marketing aspects of the business are always open to change. The strategic direction is not as crucial as the brand.

Executive Identity

The important thing about being a successful business leader in the current environment is your ability to be flexible to work with the challenges presented to you: your ability to embrace change. In many respects as butter is to bread so change is to business. It is hard to see how a business leader can be successful without continuously embracing change.

More so now than at any other time in history, we operate businesses in a revolutionary environment. We are not just dealing with a fast-changing environment, we are operating on a yearly basis with revolutionary change. Just consider that we have only had the world wide web 30 years, it is only 13 years since the first iPhone was launched, 10 years from the first iPad – all of which revolutionised customer buying patterns, channels for customer communication and the speed of communication now that we have mobile devices. It took Amazon eighteen years as a public company to catch Walmart in market value, but only two more years to double it and not least because of mobile technology.

In the Executive Identity Model®, outlined in Figure 3.13, I have identified your usual tolerance for change at the strategic, operational and product levels and I have graded these as high (H), medium (M) and low (L).

You need to be comfortable with discomfort and able to support others who are less comfortable with it. The interesting aspect of change is that there is a direct link between fear and giving up the status quo, and that is often why people are resistant to change and business leaders are no different. A business leader who is resistant to change sounds like a leader who is not really leading anymore. If this is you, then you are occupying the leadership position, but you are not leading the business onwards.

TIPS AND IDEAS

1. The following is designed to increase your awareness of actions you can take to improve your success of implementing change.
   - ✓ Create small wins to bring others with you who are not convinced the change is necessary.
   - ✓ Don't fix it if it's not broken – change should not be for change's sake.
   - ✓ Don't be afraid to change your mind if it's not working out.
   - ✓ Make sure those directly involved have the necessary training and support they will require to implement the change.
2. You should prepare your business for disaster by planning. Unplanned events can have a devastating impact on you and can even be life-changing, including poor health, the serious injury of your business partner, an accident in production or bankruptcy. So as with other issues, planning and preparation are key.

EXERCISE

Complete the following grid to assist you to mitigate business disasters.

What are the potential business disasters for you?	What will be the impact on you?	What will be the impact on the business?	What is your Plan B?

SUMMARY EXERCISE

1. Where are you on the business life cycle in Figure 3.14? Place yourself on the graph.
2. If you happen to be in your comfort zone for your Executive Identity, then complete the action plan below to take strategic actions to propel forward to the next phase.

Current Stage of Business Life Cycle	Desired Stage of Business Life Cycle	Changes Required	Completed By

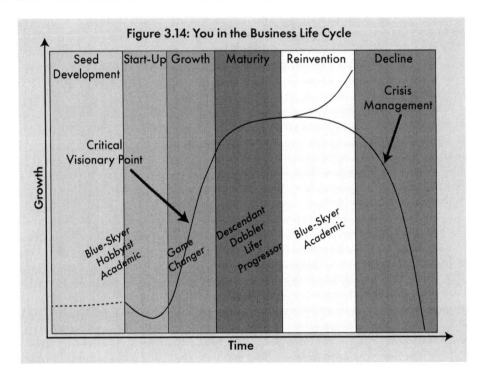

Figure 3.14: You in the Business Life Cycle

IN SUMMARY

Regardless of the stage you are currently operating in the business life cycle, the one common denominator in moving a business along and keeping it growing is the individual(s) at the helm. An individual with a clear vision backed up by skill and knowledge will steer a business through many storms. Much as with growing up, there are many aspects of business development that need nurturing – just as we do in our lives. In any business, the owner wears many, many hats and must address a range of company needs simultaneously in order to get things moving. The focus of your Executive Identity at each of these stages and the important impacts from you and on you at each juncture are vital. We owe it to ourselves to push the boundaries of our identity as far as we can and to squeeze as much out of it as we can, and to maximise its potential.

REACHING YOUR SUMMIT

4

> 'Becoming isn't about arriving somewhere or achieving a certain aim. I see it instead as forward motion, a means of evolving, a way to reach continuously toward a better self. The journey doesn't end.'
>
> Michelle Obama, *Becoming*

KEY CHAPTER POINTS

- ✓ A business leader is tasked with leading a business to be the most successful it can be.
- ✓ Maslow's Hierarchy of Needs provides a great model to examine drivers in business leadership.
- ✓ Your Executive Identity will impact on the way you lead to the summit.

Leading a business is not usually something that happens overnight. Even for the Descendant who walks into a ready-made business, it is very unlikely that they will be thrown into leadership straight away. The one and only time I witnessed this happening was when the business owner of the first generation died suddenly and his daughter was forced into the driving seat within one week, having not previously worked in the business whatsoever and grieving sorely at the death of her father. However, for most business leaders there is a gradual transition into business leadership, where skills and knowledge develop with the growth of the business. We get used to the pace but, it would seem, rarely feel fulfilled. So why is this?

Looking back at my opening paragraphs in the first chapter, I discuss the fact that business leaders are in business to succeed. I haven't yet come across anyone who has gone into business to fail. Yet, when you ask a business leader if they are satisfied with what their business (or department) has achieved – I have yet to be given a straight 'yes'. There is much written around the theory that this is because successful business leaders have a Type A personality.[5] Friedman and Rosenman (both doctors) discovered the Type A personality in their work treating cardiac patients. They identified this personality as competitive, time-urgent and an overachiever, as opposed to a Type B personality, which is relaxed, patient and easy-going. So, if we are to follow this theory to its conclusion, the attitude of the business leader means they are never quite satisfied with what they have achieved and there is always more to do.

Throughout my time in business I have often called on Maslow's Hierarchy of Needs as an excellent and well-tried way to better understand the motivation of human beings, whether self, staff, consumers, suppliers and so on. Abraham Maslow (in his 1943 paper 'A Theory of Human Motivation')[6] proposed that human needs can be organised into a hierarchy, ranging from concrete, basic needs—such as food and water—to more abstract concepts such as self-fulfilment. According to Maslow, when a lower need is met, the next need on the hierarchy becomes our focus of attention. This is illustrated in Figure 4.1.

Figure 4.1

It makes perfect sense that as humans, if we do not have food and water, we are not going to be able to think about our status, level of respect or recognition for our deeds. Maslow rightly maintains this is a luxury reserved for those who have met these basic needs. In business, this model is mostly used in marketing to understand what motivates consumers to buy. Where consumers sit on Maslow's Hierarchy of Needs will dictate the type and level of marketing used for a particular product or service. Look at what is happening with the Covid-19 global pandemic. When we enter 'lockdowns', consumers are totally focused first and foremost on their basic needs, stocking up on food and hand sanitiser to keep themselves and their families safe. We all long for the day when hand sanitiser goes back to its normal place in market demand.

As with humans, business is a living, breathing entity which makes it appropriate to apply Maslow's Hierarchy of Needs when we want to examine business leadership. Ask anyone involved in business and their view of success is when a business is fully established, thriving and generating industry-appropriate net profits. As illustrated in Figure 4.2, as business leaders we are in the driving seat to bring the business from surviving to thriving. Driving forward is as natural to a business leader as feeding is to a baby.

Figure 4.2

This diagram demonstrates how you drive the business, using your leadership, from level 1 to level 5 at the top of the triangle. In the beginning the main goal of any business is to attract adequate customers to get the business up and running, and to have enough finance to buy supplies and produce the product to keep up with customer demand. At level 2 the concern is to continue to grow the business through continued customer attraction, properly using your resources and planning ahead. At level 3 it is likely you will need others to assist you to continue to meet the growing demands of the business and to keep customer loyalty at level 4. I have superimposed the business life cycle onto Maslow's Hierarchy of Needs as there is a direct link in business terms from level 1 (start-up) to level 5 (at maturity). A business leader will need to work the business from the lower elements of the hierarchy before getting to the top of the triangle.

Imagine yourself standing at the bottom of the triangle looking upwards and needing to push the bolder in front of you to the top. The boulder is your business and your job as the business leader is to drive the business from the bottom to the top in the most effective and efficient way, using all the resources and energy at your disposal. The journey will be different depending on your Executive Identity.

BLUE-SKYER

In working with many Blue-Skyers, I have noticed that there is a common trait that you share. Although inventors, as outlined in Figure 4.3, your ambition is to get to levels 4 and 5 as quickly as possible and aim to drive the business to that point as quickly as possible. You are in a hurry to get that successful product or service out in the market. Having a recognised brand and an established business is the ultimate success. However, for you, levels 1–3 can be considered frustrating and more a means to an end – level 5 being a destination, rather than a journey. Although there is no right or wrong answer to the speed at which business leaders move through the levels, the key is that most business leaders progress through all the levels. Without attention to detail at the lower levels the foundations could become shaky.

Figure 4.3

Move quickly to Levels 4 & 5

Established business — Level 5

Recognised brand — Level 4

Team in place — Level 3

Continued business & product development through planning and resource allocation — Level 2

Some customers & adequate resources to supply your product or service — Level 1

In your impatience for success you can move forward with ideas that are not always fully formed. This can mean mistakes are made either in product development, strategic direction, recruitment or financial commitment. If this cycle happens too often your confidence in your own ability to lead can be dented.

Case in Point

I worked with an inventor of a water filter for a sports bottle a few years ago. With sales from independent retailers and sports shops creating a sustainable income for the business, the business leader was very keen to get the product into the large supermarkets and raise the profile of the brand. A keen fitness trainer, the business leader was aware there was a minor flaw in the design but so far so good. Unfortunately, when you pitch to large company buyers you don't often get a second chance, so if they don't like what they see in the first pitch it is unlikely you will get a second chance. For my client this was

> indeed the case. In his hurry to get the brand 'out there' he pushed ahead with
> the meetings with the buyers knowing there was a fundamental, albeit minor,
> design flaw. Given that large company buyers are savvy, the design flaw was
> highlighted at the meeting and the window of opportunity passed for my client.

Your impatience to succeed is not all about your leadership approach. Underlying this
can be the short-term approach to business success that is often our failsafe in Western
economies. Short-termism is a legitimate business approach and yet asks us to drive our
businesses to get financial returns as quickly as possible. The focus is on the bottom line
throughout. Within the high-tech and electronics industries this is particularly apparent.
The approach is the opposite to the Chinese business philosophy, where a business is in
place to service and support many generations. This means that strategic decisions can
be made to support a 30-year vision. I suggest there is a happy medium somewhere
in between these two approaches and as a Blue-Skyer you could take a longer-term
approach to your business growth and allow the business, like many others, to get its
full exposure to the business life cycle.

TIPS AND IDEAS

1. Discipline yourself to think in five-year cycles for your business leadership. Look
   at strategic objectives in a five-year timeframe and plan yearly accordingly.
   Others around you may try to push a shorter agenda but unless they are actual
   shareholders then you are in the driving seat. Figure 4.4 provides a useful summary.

2. Although every business needs a business plan, a business that is led by a Blue-Skyer needs a very concise working three-year plan. I suggest three years as you are likely to be in the high-growth business category and three years is probably as long as you can realistically work ahead.

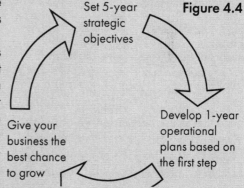

Figure 4.4

Set 5-year strategic objectives

Develop 1-year operational plans based on the first step

Give your business the best chance to grow

3. Be very clear from the outset about your business objectives and the associated
   timeframe; in other words make sure the objectives are SMART:
   S – Specific, clear and unambiguous
   M – Measurable. They must contain a number, ratio or description that makes it
   clear when and what you have achieved
   A – Achievable. Not too easy, not too hard
   R – Realistic. Must be within the capability of the business
   T – Time-bound. When must they be completed?

You should also consider how you communicate your vision to others in your team so they can also buy into what you can see and support the growth of your business. One of the best ways to do this is to involve your team in the planning process, which will enable them to have ownership and enthusiasm for the actions required.

4. Figure 4.5 provides ideas for you to drive in your business leadership.

Figure 4.5

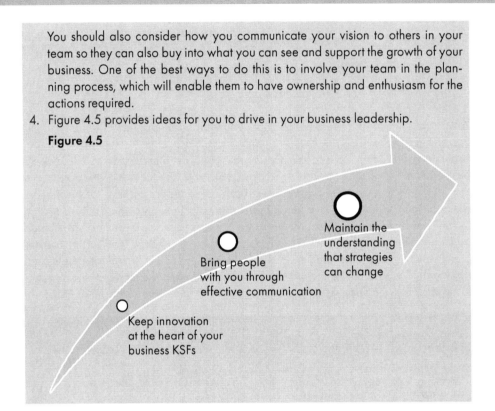

Maintain the understanding that strategies can change

Bring people with you through effective communication

Keep innovation at the heart of your business KSFs

THE DESCENDANT

Given that the previous generation has already progressed the business from levels 1 to 5 you are generally perceived to be engaged at level 5, leading the business when it's matured and established. Yet, if you think back to the business life cycle it is at this point that the business needs reinvention for its survival and further growth. So now this means that as the Descendant you need to consider your leadership from level 1 and the start-up phase. Appreciating that you will hopefully have resources and a team already in place from the previous business trading, your leadership of the business needs to take it through the reinvention stage and therefore to bring a new product or service through from level 1 again. Often described as a strategic business unit, i.e. a business within a business, the foundations need to be re-established for the reinvention.

I have always found it a challenge to advise established family businesses. Apart from the fact that there is some degree of suspicion of outsiders, the idea of reinvention is not often high on the agenda. In fact, in many circumstances there can be outright resistance to any change to either the product, the team or the customer base. As a Descendant, as illustrated in Figure 4.6, you often operate within an established

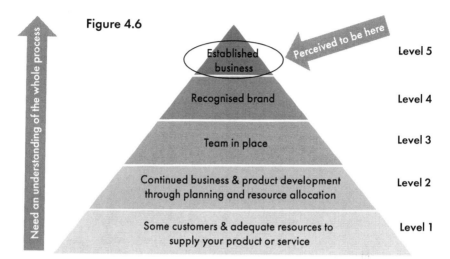

Figure 4.6

business but also need to understand what is required to lead a start-up business so that you can act as a catalyst for reinvention.

The most common leadership challenge you are most likely to have to deal with, of all the Executive Identities, is the potential dinosaurs in the business. By that I mean team members who may be resistant to doing things differently. There could be an attitude of why do we need change when it has worked perfectly well to date? As you are coming to a team and business that is already formed and has several cultural norms, some staff may not want to be disrupted during the reinvention process. It is worth noting that the main reason your colleagues are resisting change is predominantly to do with fear and to some extent their lack of confidence to embrace new concepts and ideas. By knowing this you are perhaps better equipped to understand and address their fears and provide adequate training and support to improve their confidence.

Being mentored by the current family members is an important part of developing your business leadership. Learning from the vast experience that has gone before you is a must. It is unlikely you will take everything on board all of the time, but there is a lot you can learn. You should compile your own mentoring programme that allows you to shadow and learn from each of the existing owners, making sure you cover topics such as: understanding the history and values instilled into the business by the family members; finding the approaches and competencies of exiting family members that work, operating in all functions and at all levels across the business; getting to know the business assets owned by the family.

As a business leader who has lived with your business at home as well as at work your views can reflect those who have gone before you and can be rather too subjective. This is compounded by limited leadership experience outside the business and even perhaps a limitation to your knowledge of the leadership functions. In the long run this can mean there is a preference for the status quo and a lack of reinvention. The opposite of subjectivity is objectivity and the most constructive way to counteract too much subjectivity is to introduce objectivity into your thinking.

In the past few years I have come across a few family firms that will only let the next generation come into the company after they have spent at least two years working somewhere else. I appreciate this takes a lot of bravery on everyone's part, since the new generation may like where they go and want to stay, and then what happens to the business? Yes, this is a possible risk, but business and risk go together and perhaps it is better to have a new leader who is forward-thinking regardless of whether they are from within the family or not. Maybe it needs to be about the growth of the business rather than the Descendant having to fit in.

TIPS AND IDEAS

1. There are many options to introduce objectivity into your leadership thinking and it is important these are explored. They include:
   a. Undertaking business programmes.
   b. Engaging external advisors to mentor your leadership.
   c. Working in another successful business for 12–24 months to see how others lead their businesses.
2. However odd it may seem to those around you, get yourself onto a local business start programme and teach yourself the elements of business development from start-up. This will give you an invaluable insight into the stages you need to consider for reinvention.
3. It is important not to look at change just for change's sake – there needs to be a legitimate reason for any change.
4. Explain to your team why a change may be needed and the benefits to them as individuals as well as to the business.
5. Ensure that the people involved with any change have had the appropriate training to undertake any new tasks.
6. Support your team in times of change.
7. Figure 4.7 provides a business leadership improvement cycle.
8. Figure 4.8 provides ideas to drive your business leadership.

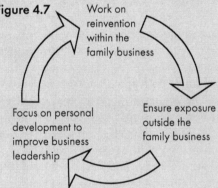

Figure 4.7

Work on reinvention within the family business

Ensure exposure outside the family business

Focus on personal development to improve business leadership

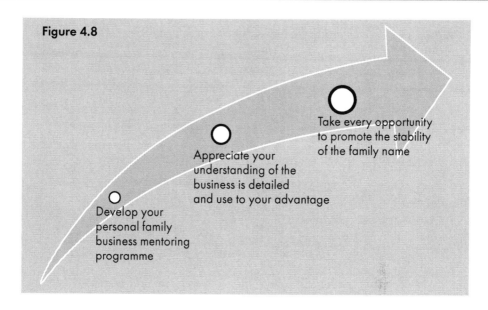

Figure 4.8

Take every opportunity to promote the stability of the family name

Appreciate your understanding of the business is detailed and use to your advantage

Develop your personal family business mentoring programme

THE HOBBYIST

Often the difficulty for the Hobbyist is seeing the level 5 vision. In many cases they even struggle to see themselves leading at level 2. As a Hobbyist, the energy it takes to move a pastime into a new business is often exhausting and as a result the business leader can spend an extraordinary amount of time at level 1. A prime example is the artisan baker who makes their bread and sells it at the local country market. Although staying at level 1 can create a lifestyle, it needs much more drive if the business is going to employ others and create a sought-after brand.

Unfortunately, as a Hobbyist your Executive Identity often holds a preconceived reputation for others that you don't really have the ambition to push the business beyond level 1 (Figure 4.9). This is especially true in the artisan sector where consumers and supporters alike believe that staying at level 1 is what makes the business artisan. There can be a reluctance to invest beyond level 1 if sales don't happen quickly enough for your returns. With a reluctance to engage in a more 'formal' business process like business planning or market analysis, you can miss the very opportunity you are seeking. The most common leadership challenge you are the most likely to have is that you are a leader who has come to business through something you have enjoyed doing and want to formalise this going forward. In some ways the idea of forming a business was secondary to your desire to work on your hobby. The process of business start-up is most likely to have evolved over time. In theory, all businesses are set up by someone; however, as the Hobbyist you are the most likely of all the leadership identities to remain the main person and focus of the business throughout its life cycle. You are the most likely to spend a lot of your business years producing your product or your

Figure 4.9

Established business	Level 5
Recognised brand	Level 4
Team in place	Level 3
Continued business & product development through planning and resource allocation	Level 2
Some customers & adequate resources to supply your product or service	Level 1

Work on growth

service. In that respect your skills, knowledge and ability are very much the dictator of business development and growth.

Throughout my years of advising businesses, the Hobbyist is the one leading a business that is less likely to grow beyond a micro business (10 employees or fewer) because the skills of the leader are generally underdeveloped. In fact, some of the Hobbyists I have worked with believe that dealing with 'business' issues takes them away from what they should really be doing – working on production and meeting customers! The other problem with this situation is that when there are unexpected changes in the business you can find it hard to navigate your way through.

You effectively manage the business single-handedly and the business relies on you for virtually all decisions, large and small. As a Hobbyist you usually find yourself trapped – because you solve the firm's everyday problems and as such you are continually presented with everyday problems. It's a vicious circle. You will spend most of your time firefighting and resolving routine tasks. By the end of the working day, you may feel you have done a day's work, but all of the strategic planning for the firm's future remains firmly on the back burner. Recruiting staff represents a step-change in growth and undoubtedly helps with sales, production and the problem of managing routine tasks such as bookkeeping.

A greater depth of business leadership is needed to take the business forward to the next stage. As well as developing your own skills, you need to think about recruiting and training others to assume managerial roles.

I really do want you to give yourself permission to move beyond this stage, if that is where you want to go. You have as much right to move your business to a global brand as any other business leader. What makes you any less of a driver in business than anyone else? There are some excellent examples where Hobbyists, particularly in the fashion industry, have gone on to create an established global brand – including the likes of Donatella Versace and Vera Wang, to name but a few. Keep these at the forefront of your mind.

TIPS AND IDEAS

1. The key to unlocking level 2 is to get beyond the hobby and start to really consider the business.
2. Doing so involves thinking outside the box. As an example, I want you to consider the following, where business leaders are asked to join the nine dots using four straight lines without lifting the pen off the paper (retracing a line counts as two lines):[7]

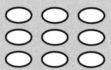

   The moral of the story is you need to think outside the box and use all the space and resources available to you.
3. It is a good idea to seek out a business advisor or potential business investor to work with you on a detailed business plan. At a minimum this needs to cover:
   a. The product or service
   b. Marketing and sales
   c. Your markets and competitors
   d. Your operations
   e. Financial forecasts
   f. The team needed
4. The cycle in Figure 4.10 provides a summary to improve your business leadership.
5. Figure 4.11 provides ideas for you to increase your leadership propulsion.

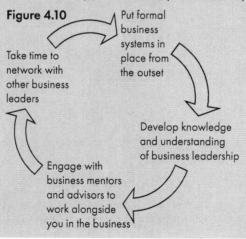

Figure 4.10

Put formal business systems in place from the outset

Develop knowledge and understanding of business leadership

Engage with business mentors and advisors to work alongside you in the business

Take time to network with other business leaders

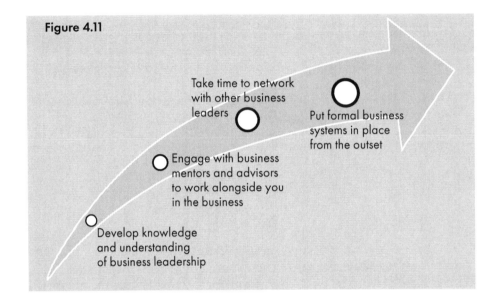

Figure 4.11

THE DABBLER

The Dabbler inherently expects to work through the levels, methodically and in order. Generally, as a Dabbler you are keen to see a 'traditional' approach to business progression and lead the business through all five levels, as illustrated in Figure 4.12. Given that you can be a little risk adverse, you may tend to linger too long at the lower levels, looking for reassurance to further invest. Importantly by not gearing up quickly enough you can give others an entry into your market and consequently lose any competitive edge you may have.

Figure 4.12

The Dabbler is often known to stay on level 3 a little longer than necessary and to be unsure of whether to employ staff to assist with the growth of the business even after significant planning. Of course, investing in employees is a major step in any business and needs to get attention, but the length of deliberation shouldn't be to the detriment of business growth.

As the Dabbler you are in business leadership in some ways to 'see what happens'. It would be good if the business gave you some healthy returns, but equally if it's not working too well then you would be content to place your energy elsewhere. It is most likely you have already gained a lot of career experience elsewhere before coming to business leadership and this is not insignificant. However, as you are the Dabbler you may lack the industry knowledge for the business you are now leading and therefore you are relying on others for their industry expertise. Clearly, as a leader of this business it is in your interests to get an understanding of the industry at least at a strategic level. Extensive networking and a curious nature are essential so that you have at least a basic knowledge of the environment you are operating in.

If it is you as the business owner and your employees are the industry experts, then this can be a difficult business situation to lead as you can feel vulnerable and dependent on others. A typical example is when the Dabbler owns a restaurant without knowing how to cook and is reliant on chefs to make or break their business. I have come across a few situations where Dabblers have been content with this scenario as they believed their leadership was about running the business rather than 'doing' the production. This is fine where you have two partners in the business with equal shareholding and an equal amount invested. This is also true for business angels who invest in an industry expert and provide strategic input but let the industry expert deal with the day-to-day management. In fact, this combination of skills, knowledge and experience can be a winning formula.

The other option you should consider is having a 'buying-in' scheme for key members of staff. This is likely to involve offering a small shareholding in the business to keep key staff invested and loyal, and also to recognise their significant contribution to the overall growth and success of the business.

The other scenario where I have seen this work is when the business brand is bigger than the industry experts employed in the business. The role of the Dabbler is to put processes, procedures and standards in place in the business so that everyone is working to that 'operating manual'. In many ways the business is led as if it is a franchise even though it's not. Your leadership is more about monitoring and policing the success of this approach.

Appreciating your investment in the business is not a bottomless pit, maximising your experience and knowledge for business growth is crucial. It is a good idea to have a specific financial investment ring-fenced for your input and stick to it. Remember though that your investment could well leverage other investors or lenders so that you multiply your funding.

TIPS AND IDEAS

1. As soon as your business can no longer be run with the existing staff levels or there are obvious skills shortages, undertake a skills gap analysis.
2. Prioritise and complete this within a short timeframe. Weeks rather than months.
3. Write your job specifications and get recruiting.
4. Figure 4.13 is a summary cycle to improve your business leadership.

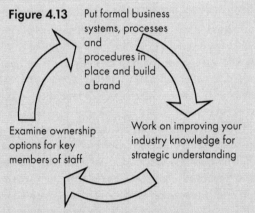

Figure 4.13   Put formal business systems, processes and procedures in place and build a brand

Work on improving your industry knowledge for strategic understanding

Examine ownership options for key members of staff

5. Figure 4.14 provides ideas to drive your business leadership.

Figure 4.14

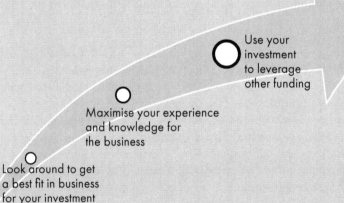

Use your investment to leverage other funding

Maximise your experience and knowledge for the business

Look around to get a best fit in business for your investment

EXERCISE

1. Complete the following table to help you examine the existing skills in your business and the skills needed that will enable it to reach its objectives.

Business Objective	Current Related Skills	Additional Skills Required

2. Use the following headings to create a basic job specification for any new positions.
   a. Job title
   b. Renumeration
   c. Essential requirements to undertake the role
   d. Main duties
   e. Responsibilities
   f. Location

THE LIFER

Like the Dabbler, your expectation is to work through each of the levels that push a business forward to maturity. The difference between you and the Dabbler is that you are anxious to get to level 5 as quickly as possible, as shown in Figure 4.15. Understanding

Figure 4.15

that you are in business to succeed, this is not surprising. The problem is that in your rush you may get impatient with the plateau that often occurs around level 3. There is a team in place but getting to a recognised brand will take significant energy and resources. This 'plateau' is often caused by your own business leadership.

As the Lifer you are a strong entrepreneurial leader who will have led your business from an idea and been involved in every aspect of its growth. A little like a parent seeing their child off to university, you may often find it difficult to let go. It is easy to give into the temptation to look over your managers' shoulders and interfere with their decisions. Of course, you know the business inside out and you may well be right when you make suggestions or overrule someone else. The problem is that you are demotivating your management team and wasting their talent, and ultimately holding your business back. Even if each individual decision you make is correct, the cumulative effect undermines your managers and harms overall business performance. And by continuing to check every detailed decision, you're also failing to free up your own time to focus on strategic issues.

The key issue for you as the Lifer is not so much skills as attitude. You need a high level of management skills and the confidence to stand back from routine management. You need to learn to let go and when to involve others and appreciate their input. You should spend a significant part of your time on strategy and developing plans for the future. You are really the only one who can take your business forward and you need to be networking aggressively with businesses, customers, suppliers, etc. to keep up to date with a changing market and looking to the next stage of your business growth.

By putting regular performance reviews in place, you will be well-informed of the internal needs of the business as well as keeping your strategy on track. Use your high levels of energy to your advantage. Motivation for success can be contagious to those around you and encourage others to put that little bit more into making the business a success. Through your desire to succeed you can move others in your team from an indifferent attitude to one that is committed to the goals of the business. To really maximise this quality, it is important you lead by example with your team, funders and key stakeholders and keep in mind the saying 'come to me with the solution to the problem, not just the problem'. You could also find there is generally less sickness absence or employee turnover when team members are valued and motivated. By harnessing that enthusiasm and bringing others with you, your business has a good chance of reaching growth and reinvention.

TIPS AND IDEAS

1. When recruiting your senior managers, you could look for ways to check out the tenacity of your team members by asking them how they have turned challenges into opportunities. This way you create a culture of staying power in the business.
2. Figure 4.16 provides a summary cycle to support your business leadership.

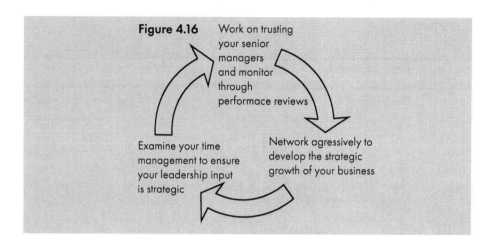

Figure 4.16

Work on trusting your senior managers and monitor through performace reviews

Network agressively to develop the strategic growth of your business

Examine your time management to ensure your leadership input is strategic

A Spotlight on the Lifer

The key question is whether a Lifer is driven forward by nature or nurture; were you born an entrepreneur or does your life experience bring you to this path? There are many, many theories surrounding this debate and, like numerous others, I happen to think it's a bit of both. Your long-term desire to make a business succeed is probably part of your DNA, combined with circumstances that led you to where you are today. Your worst nightmare would be to try in business, perhaps several times, and ultimately not reach the maturity level in business with any of your ideas.

Be aware that developing a business plan is not always something you see as relevant. However, it is. You, more than any of the other Executive Identities, need to ensure that you do not let your tenacity and determination overshadow the need to give an idea a chance in the business life cycle. There are some failsafes you can put in place to protect yourself and the business:

1. Seek other professional input to your ideas and business, and listen to the responses.
2. Strike a balance between tenacity and negative cash flows. Negative cash flow can only be sustained for a short timeframe.
3. Make sure you are adequately resourced from the outset.
4. Embrace 'formal' business processes like business planning, customer analysis, market testing and so on.
5. Work with the bodies and educational institutions in your area to improve your product development or the skills mix in your team.

THE PROGRESSOR

Experience shows that you see the vision of the established business, but the graft required in levels 1 to 4 can be very difficult. Having already worked in the industry in an established business you perhaps have an expectation of an easier process. Even with your knowledge of the industry, driving a business to the top of the triangle in Figure 4.17 will require a lot of work and long hours. This is most relevant in your case, as you are likely to have left behind an important competitor in your industry and possibly locality, in your previous employer. It is likely that you may have had a honeymoon period when your business was first established. Customers may have drifted to you to see how the new offering compares to the existing service at your old employer. It is likely that a large percentage of these customers will not remain with you and like any other new start-up you need to work hard to get new customers. As a Progressor your biggest challenge is to drive the business through the levels with tenacity and innovation, and to stop comparing your business to the one you left.

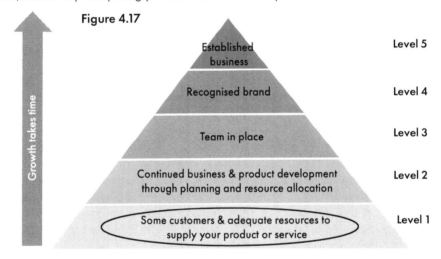

Figure 4.17

As the Progressor you have moved through your career and likely have a number of years' experience at senior management in your industry. This is a good grounding for business leadership, but it is also lacking in some essentials. Most importantly, although you are likely to have supplier and customer contacts in the industry, you may have had limited exposure to business leadership functions. As a previous 'deputy' you are also likely to lack your own strategic business contacts and need to rectify this.

There is no doubt that business leadership is like a lot of other walks in life; there is a business leaders' network that is different to a managers' network. You have now moved to leadership from management and will have baggage that a new business start leader does not have to carry. You are likely to feel that at a number of levels. You want to gain respect as a leader and be recognised as a leader, rather than a manager. Some of your new networks will have links to your previous business leader and may have issues with engaging with you, particularly if your exit from your previous employment was in any way acrimonious. This is also compounded as our business development agencies can be reluctant to give you much support as they believe you are really just displacing jobs from one business to another, without really generating any new employment, especially if your business operates in a similar geographical area.

That all said, you have moved into business leadership and you now need to move forward with purpose to succeed in your quest. Importantly, you need to gather your own strategic business network around you. You also need to develop your business knowledge and expertise, and work with other mentors and advisors to support you in building confidence in your leadership decisions. If you are not funded for this activity then you need to build it into your expenditure plan as it is as important to the growth of your business as marketing, promotion or any other business function. Its importance is often underestimated by the Progressor, so I hope I have emphasised the crucial role it has to play in your success.

TIPS AND IDEAS

Figure 4.18 is a summary cycle of the ways you can drive your business leadership forward.

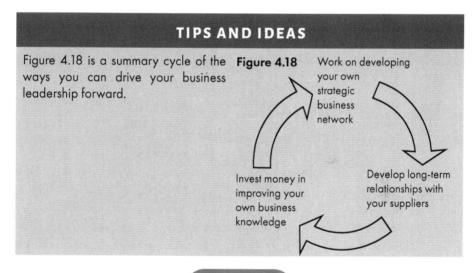

Figure 4.18

Work on developing your own strategic business network

Develop long-term relationships with your suppliers

Invest money in improving your own business knowledge

Case in Point

I worked with a Progressor many years ago who was a manager in a long-established and well-known recruitment business. Wanting to set up on his own, he approached me for start-up advice. Within the recruitment industry this activity is not unusual. Recruitment companies will protect themselves by having timeframes and geographic restrictions in their managers' contracts to mitigate too much competition. The entrepreneur in front of me was not breaching any terms of his contract, but he did have rather a rose-tinted perspective on how quickly he could create a thriving business. After revisiting his business plan, he went off to get financial backing to get set up. I keep in touch with him to this day and fifteen years later he would agree that he now has a thriving business, but his original timeline of three years was way off the mark. He often comments on our first conversation when we meet up.

THE ACADEMIC

As the Academic, Figure 4.19 illustrates that your vision can be restricted to getting to levels 2 and 3. In some ways when you have a 'busy' business and a team of people around you, you can mistake this for an established business that has 'made it'. As the Academic you may struggle to understand the position your business has in the marketplace and against your competitors. Without this insight it is difficult to understand exactly how well or not your business is performing.

Figure 4.19

For this reason, you should consider benchmarking your business against other similar businesses in your industry, which can be a very insightful process. There are many databases available and many companies you can use to assist the process, depending on the industry you are in and the countries where you are trading.

As the Academic you have worked on your product development since before it was a micro-organism. The focus continues to be on the product and your theoretical knowledge of business. You are likely to have had a high level of institutional support from, for example, a university, which has become a dependent relationship. This, together with a lack of practical experience of leading a business, can hold you back. Your background in R&D may also have been insular, so your experience of working with others has been limited. In comparison to other Executive Identities, sharing your problems with others does not always come naturally.

Given that you have, or are about to, commercialise your work, you need to develop your practical business experience as quickly as possible. It really would benefit you to have a practical business mentor work alongside you for at least the first year in business (or when you reach some sticky areas along the way). By doing this you will have a knowledgeable sounding board not just in business matters, but they will also have a genuine interest in the development of your business leadership.

TIPS AND IDEAS

1. When you find your benchmarking partners you should compare and contrast the following:
   a. Where do these companies allocate their resources?
   b. What are their average sales per employee?
   c. What are their gross profits?
   d. What are their net profits?
   e. What level of returns/complaints do they have?
2. Take plenty of business advice from experts and don't allow yourself to get stuck in the circle of idea–development–idea. Know when you need to commercialise.
3. Figure 4.20 provides a summary of ideas to drive your business leadership forward.

Figure 4.20 Consider a non-academic partner for your business to help to propel it forward

Slowly move away from your dependency on institutional support

Work with a business mentor to improve your practical business leadership

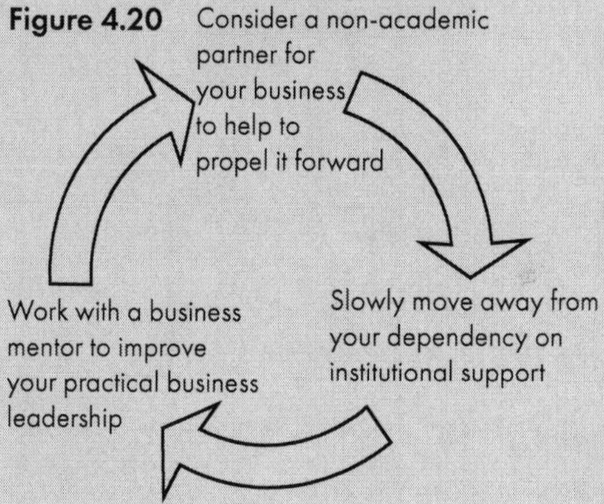

EXERCISE

Answer the following questions to begin your benchmarking process:

1. List your key business drivers. Examples might be customer care in a service business or speed of production in a manufacturing business.
2. Who are your benchmarking partners? Research your industry and you should compare your business to others of a similar make-up as well as those that are very successful in the industry.

THE GAME CHANGER

Given your Executive Identity your focus tends to be to get to level 4 as soon as possible, as shown in Figure 4.21. Brand recognition is your goal and the best indication that the cause you are championing is being understood by the masses. The recognition of your brand and the subsequent loyalty of your customers to the brand is your success. Keeping your customer loyalty through gaining their trust is your top priority. This is understandable as it takes approximately five times as much time, money and energy to attract a new customer than to keep an existing customer loyal. Customers need to know that your company and brand will do exactly as it says on the tin. Customers need to know that you are:

✓ Competent to deliver what you say you will.
✓ You will keep your promises in relation to quality, delivery and consistency.
✓ Upholding their values including sourcing your raw materials, conditions of employees in outsourced production, etc.

Figure 4.21

When consumers can recognise what your logo, tagline, name, etc. stands for, then you have achieved success. Interestingly, brand recognition can be local (the RAGE local vinyl record store in Dublin), regional (Jungle Jim's International Market in Cincinnati), national (Sol Melia, the Spanish hotel chain) or global (Apple). However, a word of caution – a brand is not sustainable unless you drive the business to the next stage of maturity and on to reinvention. You need to drive the business to the top of the triangle regardless of whether the aim is local, regional, national or global recognition. The size and scale of the business will of course be different.

As the Game Changer, your passion for your cause will certainly motivate you to give your business leadership 110 per cent. You may even consider that your enthusiasm is enough to ensure your business grows and propels forward. However, it is this very passion that can also cloud your leadership thinking to the point that it holds you back. It can also hold the business back if other key stakeholders of your business do not share your point of view, and in fact make you frustrated at their lack of vision. It is the overload of enthusiasm coupled with limited business knowledge and skills that are likely to be your obstacles.

So, as a Game Changer, you need to set aside time and resources to improve your business knowledge and expertise. This requires learning about the different stages of the business life cycle, understanding all the functions of the business in detail, working with business advisors and mentors to improve your decision-making, and making sure you network with other business leaders in a constructive way. It is important that you engage in formal business structures in the business, including business planning, management accounting, marketing and promotion to name only a few.

One of the key points about your Executive Identity in business leadership is that timing could be of the essence. Take, for example, the recent launch of the vegetarian sausage roll by the Greggs food retail chain. If that product had been launched ten years earlier, it is unlikely it would have raised interest in the local newspaper, let alone stand out as a global phenomenon. The time was right for fast-food vegetarian options to sit alongside traditional meat products. So, it is for you to be aware that the 'window of opportunity' could be the issue in launching the concept that your product represents.

TIPS AND IDEAS

1. Your desire to build a strong business on a game-changing idea will be made more successful when you recruit like-minded individuals. Your recruitment process is, however, complicated as you need to recruit individuals who have the skills and knowledge that you need in the business, as well as sharing a passion for the game-changing issue at hand. Your success is then strengthened by the synergy created in your team.

2. It is important that you call on your strengths as your key drivers to lead the business through the levels of the triangle, including your passion for your game-changing issue and the fact that you are certainly more knowledgeable about your subject than many others. You can use this to your advantage.

3. Clarify from the beginning what brand recognition you are setting out to achieve – local, regional, national or global – as this will dictate the business growth strategy.

4. Customer relations management has become a recent buzzword in business. Take time out to examine your existing customer base and brainstorm with your team how you can go the extra mile to keep their loyalty. Then check out your thinking with your customers through surveys, social media or customer feedback incentives.

5. Ensure that you lead your business built on trust so that when you agree an approach with your suppliers or customers then you will stick to it. As the saying goes, 'your word is your bond'.

6. Take time out to review your customers on a regular basis and focus on those who make the most contribution to your net profit with the least demands.

7. Set your business goals around the level of brand recognition you are aiming to achieve.

8. The other key to the success of a game-changing business is to ensure you maximise your leadership when the window of opportunity comes around.

9. Figure 4.22 is a summary cycle to assist you to drive your business leadership forward.

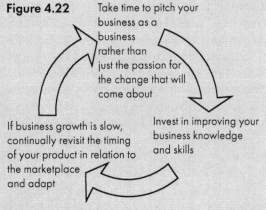

Figure 4.22

Take time to pitch your business as a business rather than just the passion for the change that will come about

Invest in improving your business knowledge and skills

If business growth is slow, continually revisit the timing of your product in relation to the marketplace and adapt

Case in Point

Love Film, a UK-based company providing DVDs by mail, was a household brand with two million subscribers in 2011. Yet without driving the business to full maturity and reinvention, the brand disappeared almost overnight with the launch of Netflix and online streaming of films. On the other hand, Ethan Brown and the establishment of Beyond Meat is an excellent example of a Game Changer who drove the business to maturity and the New York Stock Exchange. Set up in 2009 with the first ever plant-based 'meat' products, the brand started to get traction and Bill Gates invested in 2013. The company's value is estimated today at US$1.2 billion and it is a brand known all over the US and Canada.[8] This is impressive work given how niche plant-based diets were only a few years ago.

WHAT COULD POSSIBLY HOLD YOU BACK FROM REACHING YOUR SUMMIT? LET'S TALK ABOUT FEAR

What could hold you back from hitting the top of that summit in Maslow's Hierarchy of Needs? Fear of failure is the most prevalent thought that infiltrates the mind of every business leader I have ever met. Some view it as a long-term ailment that needs to be kept under control, while others view it as a constant driver that gets them out of bed every morning. In my observations, it is often the business leader who appears to have made a success of their business who can harbour the most fear. They would argue that perhaps they feel they have more to lose than others, or in the lyrics of John Denver,[9] 'The bigger they are, the harder they fall'. Regardless of your perspective, every business leader will feel fear and as with many other business leadership challenges, it's how you deal with it that matters.

Fear is an important part of business leadership, contributing to many of our decisions and actions. Interestingly, it is often fear that keeps you focused and aware of your business surroundings, every day. The dichotomy is that it can:

1. Paralyse you as only negative fear can. This is when you have unrealistic fears and they prevent you from getting to where you want to be.
2. Propel you forward and so it is a positive fear. This is the type of fear that motivates you to take informed and calculated decisions by thinking through the business problem. This type of fear can help you stay ahead of the competition or keep ahead of others by doing a better job.

So how do you know which is which? The most important thing is to recognise that fear is often referred to in leadership as a 'gut feeling' – that you know something is not quite right in the business. By paying attention and being ready for fear you can assess if it is positive or negative and whether the problem is real and needs informed attention, or just an irrational thought. Business is a lot of fun, but most of the time it is not easy.

Case in Point

When the global recession hit in 2008, I was working with a number of business leaders who had thousands of Euro stripped off their balance sheets. Their wealth went from the stratosphere to ground level within days. Many of these leaders were business colleagues and had become friends over the years, so it was a very difficult time. One in particular stands out. He was a Lifer who had a good business in distribution and had invested a lot of profits into property, especially for his retirement – so the hit was significant and much was lost. Clearly there was a lot to deal with and he entered an emotional rollercoaster for the best part of two years to deal with the fallout. However, after a few days of shutting himself off from the world, he got up and developed a strategy to deal with the circumstances and to work out a plan with his advisors to protect his business and his employees. All his leadership qualities were tested to the limit and his attitude is really what carried him and his business through. He still operates the distribution business, has had to delay his retirement, has lost one-third of his staff, but he is still here and operating and, in many respects, now has a business with much greater financial controls in place.

This case could so easily have turned into a total wipe-out for all those involved and maintaining such a strong approach is not always easy. Unfortunately, this is not an isolated case and successful business leadership can make us dig very, very deep to bring back some sort of equilibrium to our world and the world of those who depend on us.

TIPS AND IDEAS

1. Share your fears with others and get their reaction. Check out if they view your fear as positive or negative. Talk to a few people and get different perspectives – as the saying goes, 'a problem shared is a problem halved'.[10]
2. A common fear for business leaders is losing a key partner or senior member of their team through illness or death. The best way to mitigate for this is through 'keyperson' insurance. So, if you don't have this in place it might be worth some serious consideration.

EXERCISE

Whether it is fear of failure or attitudes you need to address in your Executive Identity, it is important to understand you are not alone. It is also empowering to know that they can be managed through your attention and effort, and are certainly not insurmountable. Facing your fears is one way to appreciate that you will have the attitude and capability to deal with them if they should happen. Write down your top five fears for your business leadership and then state what actions you would take to mitigate the problems. Please use the following grid to assist you and consider the other people who could help you to deal with the issues.

Top 5 fears	Actions I could take to de-escalate the problem	Who else might I involve in assisting me?
1.		
2.		
3.		
4.		
5.		

SUMMARY EXERCISE

Driving a business from surviving to thriving is challenging for any leader. Using the best of your Executive Identity to assist you, can only be a positive move. Figure 4.23 is designed to encourage you to reflect on how you can use your strengths as drivers by identifying ways to make them work for you.

Figure 4.23

Blue-Skyer	Descendant	Hobbyist	Dabbler	Lifer	Progressor	Academic	Game Changer
1. Visionary 2. Confident 3. Comfortable with risk 4. An innovator	1. You know your business well 2. You have significant 'on-the-job' learning	1. You have huge enthusiasm 2. You know your craft	1. Can take some risk with the investment 2. Time to look around for the right business idea 3. Experience to draw upon	1. High levels of tenacity & determination 2. Comfortable with business risk	1. Industry knowledge 2. Understand your customer 3. Knowledge of the supply chain	1. Sound knowledge of your product 2. Spent a number of years perfecting your product 3. Engaged with several business mentors	1. Passion for your game-changing issue 2. You are more knowledgeable about your subject than many others
List ways to make this work for you	List ways to make this work for you	List ways to make this work for you	List ways to make this work for you	List ways to make this work for you	List ways to make this work for you	List ways to make this work for you	List ways to make this work for you

In Summary

I think most of us would agree that we would prefer to thrive than merely survive. This is important for you as a business leader as well as your business. Your business wants to thrive also, but it needs you to drive it forward. Although we would want this to be a smooth process in a purposeful environment, this is rarely the case. If we examine nature, we can see that some plants do thrive in the most adverse conditions, like cacti in the desert. As a business leader you need to take a leaf out of this book and focus on the best ways you can drive your business to thrive even if the conditions are adverse. In the process you may need to overcome your fear of failure and move on.

YOUR FUNCTIONAL LEADERSHIP

'This is a story about four people named Everybody, Somebody, Anybody and Nobody. There was an important job to do and Everybody was asked to do it. Everybody was sure Somebody would do it. Anybody could have done it, but Nobody did it. Somebody got angry because it was Everybody's job. Everybody thought Anybody would do it, but Nobody realised that Everybody wouldn't do it. It ended up that Everybody blamed Somebody when Nobody did what Anybody could have done.'
C. Swindoll, founder of 'Insight for Living' broadcast

KEY CHAPTER POINTS

✓ There are three key functions – the Trio of Functions – that need to be considered by any business leader.
✓ Your Executive Identity will influence the balance of these three functions in your business leadership.
✓ The key to effective leadership is working on achieving a balance in your Trio of Functions.

A SUMMARY OF THE TRIO OF FUNCTIONS

As a business leader your business demands three main functions for you:

✓ Managerial

✓ Commercial
✓ Entrepreneurial

There are many, many, books written on these leadership functions and in fact hundreds of books for each of them individually. This chapter is concerned about the balance of this trio in relation to your Executive Identity and so I summarise them, simply by way of a reminder.

Managerial

This function focuses on getting things done by working with and through other people. This function has three key elements:

a. Planning
b. Coordinating
c. Directing

It is impossible to be a business leader without managing. Some use the analogy of a hovering helicopter. As a leader you are in the helicopter observing the business and are able to have an overview of the landscape ahead. However, there are times when you may need to land the helicopter, roll up your sleeves and get on with the management tasks at hand.

a. *Planning* – when you plan in business you are setting objectives today for the future performance across all aspects of the business. By giving yourself the time to work on the business, rather than in it, you will be up to date with a changing market and looking to the next stage of your business growth. There will always be new challenges and opportunities that you need to examine and take stock. Planning will assist you to:
   ✓ Spot potential pitfalls before they happen
   ✓ Structure the business more efficiently
   ✓ Focus your development efforts and direct your energy
   ✓ Work as a measure of your success
b. *Coordinating* – in its simplest form management is about getting things done in a business by working through another medium, whether that's people, equipment, materials or finance. It involves the effective delegation of tasks in a supportive environment.
c. *Directing* – by coordinating and directing you will be able to guide, teach and mentor employees to work efficiently and effectively to reach the business goals. This is about bringing people, equipment and resources together so that they work collectively to deliver on your business plan.

Commercial

The commercial function relates to the commercial aspects of the business and involves three main elements:

a. Production
b. Marketing
c. Finance

In essence, these are the practical nuts and bolts of any business. The commercial function is really what makes a business tick and as a business leader you need to be competent and confident in all three areas. You can of course support your knowledge and skills through the people you appoint to your team, but ultimately you need to understand the significance of all three.

a. *Production* – the production in any business relates to the premises, layout of equipment, operational processes, research and development, and product design. In some businesses this element can be highly technical or very mechanised.
b. *Marketing* – marketing is about getting your product or service into the hands of the end consumer, so they are satisfied with what they receive. This element includes consumer research, packaging, promotional activities, distribution and pricing.
c. *Finance* – the financial element is the cornerstone of any business. Just like a household, it is impossible to run a business without money. As the business leader you need to understand the investment the business needs and how best to fund it, any capital expenditure required, controlling operational expenditure and maintaining a positive cashflow.

Entrepreneurial

Although the idea of an entrepreneur probably emerged around the time of the Renaissance around the 1340s, it was only in the 1970s that the concept of an entrepreneur really started to gain traction in the business community. The entrepreneurial function has three main elements:

a. Risk-taking
b. Decision-making
c. Innovation

Many argue this is a less 'tangible' function than the commercial function. How can a business leader define or even learn risk-taking or innovation? This is often the function that the nature vs nurture debate revolves around when we speak of whether entrepreneurs are born or learn their 'trade'. Whichever way you fall in this debate is not as relevant as the fact that you need this function to lead a successful business.

a. *Risk-taking* – business leadership involves mitigating a number of different types of risks, including strategic, physical, environmental, technological, financial and human.
b. *Decision-making* – any business leader will make decisions on a daily basis. Depending on the issue these can be strategic or operational, and depend on the experience and knowledge of those around to assist.
c. *Innovation* – this element of any business is about introducing new ideas, concepts, products, methods or workflows. It can be major or minor, but the ultimate goal is to innovate to improve.

As set out in Figure 5.1, I will refer to these throughout as your Trio of Functions and they are managerial, commercial and entrepreneurial. Although there are specific circumstances that could unbalance this trio, as a business leader the goal is to maintain an overall balance.

Figure 5.1

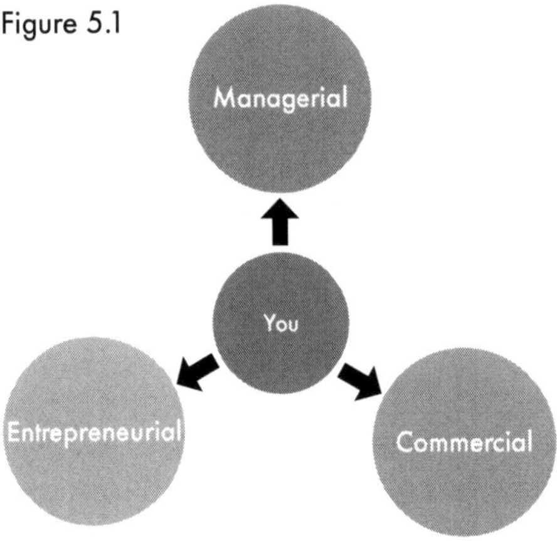

As with our health for example, if there is a prolonged imbalance between calorie input, calorie output and exercise then our health is at risk. It's the same with the health of our business. If, for example, the risk highlighted in the entrepreneurial function was to dominate too long over the finance and marketing of the commercial function, then the survival of the business could be severely compromised.

THE BLUE-SKYER

Figure 5.2 outlines the typical imbalance that exists in the Blue-Skyer when it comes to the trio of leadership functions.

As a Blue-Skyer your entrepreneurial function involving risk, decision-making and innovation is dominant over your commercial and managerial functions. As a business leader comfortable with a dominant entrepreneurial function, you can be prone to taking decisions that are not always fully informed. This can waste time as you may need to retrace your direction when a particular road runs out. Take product development as an

Figure 5.2

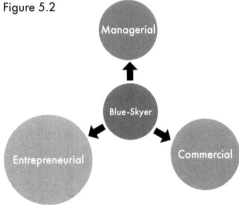

example – it stands to reason that if your product is deficient in relation to your competitors it is going to struggle to gain and keep market share. The smallest of technical issues can place your product in an inferior category to your direct competitor and with such a high level of product manufacturing being outsourced, quality management is of the essence. This is particularly relevant for the Blue-Skyer or the Academic where production is more likely to be outsourced. This is how you are naturally most comfortable in your leadership functions. It is important to appreciate that you need to work on achieving a balanced trio in order to lead your business effectively. Once a product has a reputation for inferiority in the marketplace it can be hard to come back from that space.

The most high-profile example I can think of in relation to this point is the speech by Gerald Ratner. He created such a disaster for the sale of his products it now has its own terminology on social media called 'Doing a Ratner'. Ratner was CEO of the Ratner Group – Britain's largest high-street jeweller with over 50 per cent of the UK market. In 1991 he gave a speech to an audience of 6,000 business people and journalists at an Institute of Directors convention, where he notoriously described his own company's products as 'crap'. Almost overnight the share price fell and then the business had to close 2,500 shops, after taking 30 years to build.

Your lack of attention to planning or coordinating your team to achieve business results can be missing. Figure 5.3 sets out your usual order of leadership dominance.

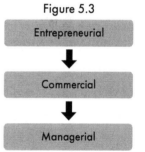

Figure 5.3

Entrepreneurial

↓

Commercial

↓

Managerial

Case in Point

A few years ago, I was working with a husband and wife partnership involved in software development for the architectural industry. The husband was an architect by trade and his wife specialised in IT and software development. When I got involved with the business it was really still at the start-up stage. Although a lot of R&D had been carried out, little had been checked out with potential customers as to the suitability of the software. The business was also running out of money, fast. We managed to get a plan in place with some realistic cash flows that enabled the business to access a decent overdraft facility from their bank. We then engaged with two potential customers to involve them in the completion of the software product design. There had to be some backtracking on this to get the product suitable but they were able to go forward and start to sell their product through licences.

TIPS AND IDEAS

Managerial

1. Develop a working three-year business plan for the business with an associated one-year operating plan. Review and revise annually.
2. Undertake a skills gap analysis.
3. Get involved in the recruitment of new staff.
4. Put a performance review system in place for staff with target setting and associated training.

Commercial

1. Understand how to read a set of accounts.
2. Put a monthly management accounting system in place and use it.
3. Work with others to examine the best production process for your business.
4. Continually seek customer feedback on your product or service.
5. Continually scan your marketplace for innovation and developments.
6. Undertake the exercise set out next to examine the appropriateness of your premises.

Entrepreneurial

1. Taking risks can be addictive so if your innovation has traction, move to the growth stage of the business within a reasonable time.
2. Train yourself to make more informed strategic decisions by taking more time, gathering different types of information and thinking through the pros and cons.
3. Create 'blue sky' thinking time in your business where all ideas are gathered and discussed. This can be ring-fenced to avoid it always seeping into business functions.

EXERCISE

The following is designed to assist you with an important aspect of your managerial function – business planning. Draft up a ten-page business plan for the next three years of your business using the following headings:

✓ An executive summary – an overview of the business. Many lenders and investors make judgements about your business based on this section of the plan alone
✓ A short description of the business opportunity – who you are, what you plan to sell or offer, why and to whom
✓ Your marketing and sales strategy – why you think people will buy what you want to sell and how you plan to sell to them
✓ Your management team and personnel – your credentials and the people you plan to recruit to work with you

✓ Your operations – your premises, production facilities, management information systems and IT

✓ Financial forecasts – this section translates everything you have said in the previous sections into numbers

A business plan is a written documentation of your business development and should be a live document that gets updated on a regular basis. Regularly updating your business plan is a good way to keep your strategy on track; you should review it every six months.

THE DESCENDANT

Figure 5.4 outlines the typical imbalance that exists in the Descendant when it comes to the trio of leadership functions.

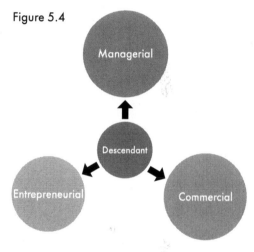

Figure 5.4

As a Descendant both your managerial function involving planning, coordinating and directing and your commercial function of finance, management and operations are well honed. Probably one of the key factors that can affect your business leadership is the naysayers on your team who may resent a new approach from the 'new kid on the block' – literally. As the Descendant you need to sieve out those with a genuine interest in your success against those who really have nothing better to do with their time and your energy.

As a business leader with a subordinate entrepreneurial function you can be lacking in innovation and idea generation. Figure 5.5 sets out your usual order of leadership dominance.

Figure 5.5

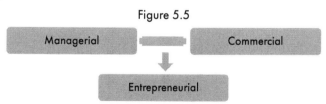

This is how you are naturally most comfortable in your leadership functions. It is important to appreciate that you need to work on achieving a balanced trio in order to lead your business effectively.

TIPS AND IDEAS

Managerial

1. Examine the skills mix in the business against the mix required to reach the business objectives, and address any gaps through recruitment, training and mentoring.
2. Ensure there are monthly senior management meetings to assist communication.
3. Champion your projects in the business to gain recognition of leadership outside of other family members.

Commercial

1. Make sure you are provided with the financials of the business.
2. Develop your own relationships with key stakeholders to the business, including your accountant, bank manager and solicitor.
3. Regularly reach out to your customers and understand how your product or service meets a need in the marketplace.
4. Understand all aspects of the business from frontline services to strategic decision-making.

Entrepreneurial

1. Make time for innovation in the business. Examine how you can encourage staff to come forward with new ideas for product, production, design, operations, customers, etc.
2. Ensure that you are making operational and strategic decisions in the business to build up your reputation with suppliers and staff.
3. Ensure you are included in all financial decisions in the business.

EXERCISE

The following is designed to assist you with an important aspect of your entrepreneurial function – promoting innovation. To be a creative business leader you need to take other ideas on board – you don't know which one might turn out to be the winner. The following is a mind map technique you can use with other team members to brainstorm new approaches to a problem. The key is for you to identify the problem and then let everyone contribute their solutions without any filtering. Figure 5.6 only goes as far as six ideas but I suggest this could be 106.

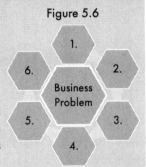

Figure 5.6

This creates a real culture of ideas generation when used with team members on a regular basis.

THE HOBBYIST

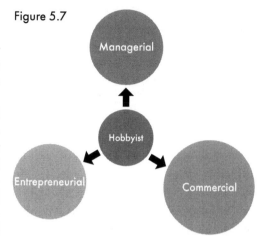

Figure 5.7

Figure 5.7 outlines the typical imbalance that exists in the Hobbyist when it comes to the trio of leadership functions.

As a Hobbyist your commercial function involving production, marketing and finance is dominant over your entrepreneurial and managerial functions. As a business leader comfortable with a dominant commercial function, you can be prone to focusing exclusively on the production of your product. This is not surprising given that your business is built on your craft and passion for your craft. As you can tend to remain as a sole trader or micro business (employing fewer than ten people) there is a limited focus on your managerial function.

You also need to consider your location. Working from home can be a very convenient way for many Hobbyists to conduct their business. It has many positives for a number of people, in particular those who are starting out and those who are sole traders. For those of you who work from home you understand it also has many downsides, including the demands on you to put on a load of washing in between your phone calls. A business needs a place to operate from that is appropriate for its needs. If you are a Hobbyist and have been selling clothes online at the weekends you likely had no issues storing your goods in your living room for a few weeks. However, if you are now selling goods online as your career and operating out of a studio apartment you are going to run out of space very quickly. Although working from home can be comforting and convenient, like recruiting your first employee, committing to a regular rent and rates overhead is one of the junctures of commitment an entrepreneur will make. Paying for a regular (and often substantial) overhead says you are taking this seriously. In reality if a business can't sustain this overhead my question is – is it really a business or is it still a hobby?

With so many inexpensive business spaces to rent at present I think this is ultimately a personal choice. If, however, the business could expand if it moved out of your home, then your premises are definitely holding you back.

Figure 5.8 sets out your usual order of leadership dominance. This is how you are naturally most comfortable in your leadership functions. It is important to appreciate that you need to work on achieving a balanced trio in order to lead your business.

Figure 5.8

Commercial

Managerial   Entrepreneurial

TIPS AND IDEAS

Managerial

1. Develop a three-year business plan to grow your business and review every six months.
2. Identify a 'significant other' to act as your sounding board, solely for business functions.
3. If you are a sole trader make sure to use your business network wisely to gain knowledge and confidence to grow your business

Commercial

1. Examine at least one new way to sell to your customer – it could be wholesale, online, a new retail outlet, etc.
2. Understand how to read your financial accounts and use them to make informed business decisions.
3. Make sure you take a decent salary from your business. If a business cannot support you to live then, really, why are you in business? You cannot survive otherwise; much like a parent, if you cannot nurture your child the child is unlikely to survive.
4. Ensure you are located on the best premises in the best location for your business to thrive.

Entrepreneurial

1. Ask your customers for feedback on your products, either directly or through social media, and use this information to improve your products, branding, customer service, etc.
2. Research new ways to build, present or sell your products. Involve an external point of view – maybe through your local college or university R&D facilities.

EXERCISE

The following is designed to assist you with an important aspect of your entrepreneurial function – risk. By working your way from levels 2 to 4 you are effectively growing your business through product development. Complete the table on the right-hand side with options on how you could satisfy levels 2 to 4 given that level 1 is your current position.

As a Hobbyist if you have not yet considered level 2 then this is a must to encourage the first step in the growth of your business.

Increasing Level of Risk ↑

| Level 4 – New Products into New Markets |
| Level 3 – New Products into Existing Markets |
| Level 2 – Existing Products into New Markets |
| Level 1 – Existing Products into Existing Markets |

THE DABBLER

Figure 5.9 outlines the typical imbalance that exists in the Dabbler when it comes to the trio of leadership functions.

As a Dabbler your commercial and managerial functions are dominant over your entrepreneurial function. As a business leader who has experience of the business or organisational environment you are usually comfortable with the elements of management and commercial business operations. You can tend to focus on these functions and can be less comfortable with business risk as you may also have your own agenda for business involvement.

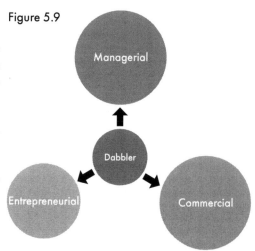

Figure 5.9

The key is also to ensure that you don't micro-manage an experienced team just because you believe that your experience can be superior. Like customers, your staff needs to know they can trust you to lead them in the right direction to ensure their job security and to be there when things can be tough for them. Yet it doesn't stop there. It is your job as business leader to also ensure there is trust among your team members. In many ways a team without trust is not really a team. When team members trust each other they will open up, generate new ideas, support each other and genuinely want the best for team PLC. The needs of the team will become more important than the needs of the individual.

This is not always an easy environment to create but for those business leaders who strike this atmosphere the rewards both as a business leader and as an individual are high. One of the simplest ways for you to gain the trust of your team is to let them get to know you and understand you as a person and a business leader. People trust people they know and understand – it's human nature. Just think of your friendships; your closest friends are the ones you know and understand the best, the ones you trust. Sharing your history will encourage your team to be more open and honest. Try this as it does work. The time and energy required to lead staff who are disgruntled and discontent is draining.

Figure 5.10 sets out your usual order of leadership dominance.

Figure 5.10

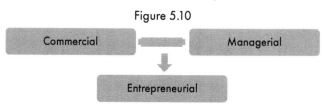

Case in Point

I once worked with a business leader who was a full-time teacher and also owned a women's clothes shop as well as a car wash depot. The owner wanted to leave his full-time position and operate his businesses. However, neither business was doing particularly well and the business leader was convinced there were more efficient ways the businesses could run, and asked if I would have a look. His teaching job was 15 kilometres away from his businesses and he would drive those 15 kilometres every lunchtime, every day, to check on each business and then drive 15 kilometres back to his work. He would then finish his teaching day and go to finish off his working day at each business. Apart from the fact that he was exhausted and not really making the best business decisions, he also employed and paid well for a competent manager in each business. The problem was they were not allowed to manage, and every time they tried to use their vast experience it was undermined by the owner. They, of course, were totally demotivated. The most important change to allow the businesses to grow was to encourage the business leader and his managers to develop their business plans and agree on targets that could be measured. The business owner also found a café close to his school that he enjoyed eating in and would go there for lunch most days, leaving his managers to get on with their job. The last time I looked the businesses were beginning to grow.

This is how you are naturally most comfortable in your leadership functions. It is important to appreciate that you need to work on achieving a balanced trio in order to lead your business effectively.

TIPS AND IDEAS

Managerial

1. With your experience you have a real opportunity to develop your team using your own mentoring skills so ensure these are developed and up to date.
2. Consider the idea of 'selligating' rather than 'delegating'; in other words when handing over a task be sure to 'sell' the benefits to the individual as well as the business. This approach enables both you and the member of your team to reflect on the purpose of the task and to understand when it's completed. You then need to trust that the task will be done effectively and efficiently.

Commercial

1. Examine your own skills mix and be honest. Make sure and recruit to cover any gaps you find, either on a full-time, part-time or consultancy basis.
2. Using your experience, make sure your internal workflow operations are the best and most efficient they can be.

3. Ask for customer feedback on a regular basis and listen to it, making changes accordingly.
4. Understand how to read a set of accounts.

Entrepreneurial

1. Regularly review the risks in your business and build in contingencies to cover these. Risks can include: competitor action; commercial issues – sales, prices, deliveries; operations; IT; and staff – skills, availability and costs.
2. Incorporate some 'free thinking' into the business on a regular basis to allow your staff to contribute to ideas generation for business improvement.

EXERCISE

The following is designed to assist you to understand your perspective on an important aspect of your entrepreneurial function – decision-making. Please rate yourself against each question with 1= not at all and 5= absolutely.

Demands	Rating 1–5
How well do you handle uncertainty?	
How positive is your attitude?	
How much are you prepared to take chances and gamble on your ideas?	
Do you have any of the key qualities of a typical entrepreneur?	
Do you have an absolute determination to succeed?	
Can you bounce back from setbacks?	
Are you able to delegate?	
Do you have core business skills?	
Are you prepared to spend time carrying out in-depth market research?	
Do you have sufficient funds to set aside?	

Those categories you have rated a 1 or 2 you should work on to improve your business leadership approach.

THE LIFER

As a Lifer you are the Executive Identity we all typically consider a business leader. Comfortable with all three functions and working them in a balanced way, Figure 5.11 demonstrates that you generally have a balanced trio of leadership functions.

As a Lifer you do not tend to have a dominant function overall. However, you are likely to have dominant functions depending on the situation and circumstances of

the business at a particular point in time. **Figure 5.11**
Figure 5.12 sets out your usual order of
leadership as equal and balanced.

This is how you are naturally most
comfortable in your leadership functions. Usually you do not need to work
on achieving a balanced trio but rather
on maintaining it, even during the more
challenging times in business. Your
biggest issue is your tendency to work in
isolation with all the major strategic decisions. Although you may engage others
in your decision-making processes, you

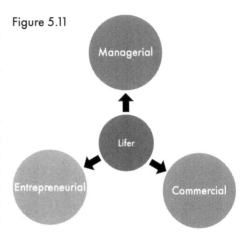

Figure 5.12

| Managerial | ⬌ | Commercial | ⬌ | Entrepreneurial |

have a tendency not to actively listen and as such may miss some crucial detail and
information. As a Lifer you need to practice active strategy development.

In larger businesses, successful management is a complex balancing act and you
need to lead and motivate your management team, spending a significant part of your
time on strategy and developing plans for the future. This requires a high level of management skills and the confidence to stand back from routine management. As a Lifer
you are well placed to take your business forward, but you need to give yourself the
time to work on the business, rather than in it. This will allow you to be up to date with a
changing market and looking to the next stage of your business growth.

Your ability to grow from disappointment and turn a failure into a success helps
your team to look beyond the immediate adversity. Tenacity is particularly important
because it means you place the long-term vision well beyond the short-term difficulties
and so you are less likely to get diverted from the task at hand – the success of your
business.

TIPS AND IDEAS

Managerial

1. Actively engage with your senior managers on a regular basis. You may be most
   comfortable with taking all the strategic decisions, but they can offer you some
   very important input.
2. Regular performance reviews and updates of your business plan are good ways
   to keep your strategy on track.

Commercial

1. Ensure you engage with the operational level of the commercial function and not just the strategic, where you like to focus.
2. Personally attend at least one trade show for your industry per year, so that you can keep up to date with trends.

Entrepreneurial

1. Examine ways to enable your team to regularly address innovation, whether that's new product design, branding, work patterns or methods.
2. Practice decision analysis, i.e. look at your problem from other angles and see if you still come up with your original decision rather than jumping in too quickly.
3. Although instincts are an important part of leading a business, it is crucial you examine risks in detail and always have a plan B.

EXERCISE

The following is designed to assist you with an important aspect of your managerial function – engaging your team through a basic performance review system. Please complete the following questionnaire in relation to your senior management team (this could be one deputy or a number of departmental heads).

	Quarterly	6-Monthly	Yearly	Not at All	How effective is this approach on a scale of 1–5 (1 = not effective, 5= very effective)
How often do you discuss your senior managers' individual performances?					
How often do you set individual targets for your senior managers?					

How often do you examine the training needs of your senior managers?				
How often do you mentor your senior managers in new skills or tasks?				

Where you are not scoring at least a 4 in each category, I suggest you need to give this leadership requirement some additional time and space. Without you, as the business leader, taking an interest in your senior managers there really is no one else.

THE PROGRESSOR

Figure 5.13 outlines the typical imbalance that exists in the Progressor when it comes to the trio of leadership functions.

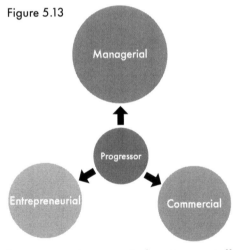

Figure 5.13

As a Progressor, your managerial function involving planning, coordinating and directing is dominant over your commercial and entrepreneurial functions. It is not surprising that this is the balance of your trio, given that a substantial part of your experience has been in a managerial role. As the deputy in another business or organisation you will have developed significant managerial skills. However, as a business leader comfortable with a dominant managerial function, you can be prone to focusing on staff coordination and direction, while there is a lack of attention to strategic decision-making, innovation, marketing, pricing and finance.

Getting your product price right is really a building block for any successful business and particularly for the Progressor, as you are the most likely to be in a price-competitive market and possibly with your previous employer. There are really four considerations you need to give attention to when it comes to pricing:

✓ You clearly need to cover your costs
✓ It needs to be set so that the business can make a profit

✓ The price needs to reflect the image of the business and the brand
✓ It needs to be acceptable to the customer and compare favourably to the competition

So, if you work on covering your costs with an acceptable profit margin for your industry and you are well above the price of your nearest competitor, the product price will hold you back in leading a successful business.

Figure 5.14 sets out your usual order of leadership dominance. This is how you are naturally most comfortable in your leadership functions. When you first get into business leadership you can be taken by surprise at the number and level of functions you need to lead. It is important to appreciate that you need to work on achieving a balanced trio in order to lead your business effectively.

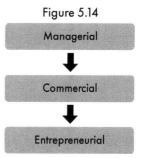

Figure 5.14

Managerial

Commercial

Entrepreneurial

TIPS AND IDEAS

Managerial

1. Examine ways that you can delegate some of your managerial elements to others, especially the things you like doing (maybe staff rotas?) and release up time for you to focus on the other business functions.
2. Focus on a more strategic approach to this function and develop a working three-year business plan for the business with an associated one-year operating plan. Review and revise yearly.

Commercial

1. Understand how to read a set of accounts and use the information to improve your business.
2. Set up a monthly management accounting system to better support your operational control and decisions.

Entrepreneurial

1. You need to get comfortable with making strategic business decisions. The most effective way to do this is to bring in an external mentor to assist you in this process until you are more confident with your approach.
2. Introduce regular brainstorming sessions into the business with your staff. Enable them to put across ideas of new ways to do things. Importantly, in the filtering process that follows you do need to manage expectations so that the new ideas are not beyond the financial ability of the business.

EXERCISE

The following is designed to assist you with an important aspect of your managerial function – financial control. Please use this checklist as a guide and ensure all the suggestions are completed within three months from today.

Action Item	Completed
Review your budgets and set realistic and achievable targets for the next year.	
Review debtors list and chase up overdue invoices.	
Offer existing debtors extended payment terms and/or discounts.	
Make sure your terms of business contain explicit payment terms.	
Assign responsibility to one individual for invoicing and collections.	
If appropriate, review banking facilities and discuss future needs.	
Put extra effort into making sure your relationships with your better customers are solid.	
Review and flowchart the main processes in your business (e.g. sales processing, order fulfilment, shipping) and challenge the need for each step.	
Encourage team members to suggest ways to streamline and simplify processes (e.g. sit down and brainstorm about efficiencies and cost reduction).	
Get your members of staff involved in a discussion of likely trading conditions and get their input on reducing costs and maintaining revenues.	
Review your list of products and services, and eliminate those that are unprofitable or not core products/services.	
Establish your KPIs and measure them on a monthly basis, e.g. sales leads generated, orders supplied/fulfilled, cash balance, stock turnover, debtor days, gross profit and net profit.	

THE ACADEMIC

Figure 5.15 outlines the typical imbalance that exists in the Academic when it comes to the trio of leadership functions.

As the Academic you have spent a great deal of time in the educational environment and as such may have areas that need to be developed in all three leadership functions. Through your extensive mentoring support, you are very likely to have a good knowledge of the elements of effective managerial, commercial and entrepreneurial functions in theory, and you just need to put them into practice. It is also likely that you have relied on your academic contacts to find a physical space for your business that was easy but not necessarily the best location or set-up for your business to grow. It could even be an incubation space where you really do outstay your welcome after the first 18 months and definitely the first two years.

There is nothing like inappropriate premises to hold your business back.

Figure 5.15

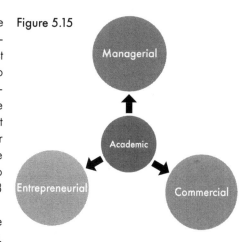

Moving premises can be an expensive activity and so it is one of those obstacles that doesn't get the attention it deserves when it needs to get done. Often I have seen sticking plaster solutions to try to make an existing premises support expansion when it is clearly not fit for purpose. Clearly you need to detail the costs and the rate of return to recuperate those costs, but that is not the whole picture. Not moving to create the space for that additional piece of machinery, or additional staff, means that not only are you not generating the potential increase in sales, you may not be able to satisfy the demands of your existing customers, and worse of all you may be giving your competitors an edge and start to lose market share. The loss can be catastrophic to the business.

As much as I am an advocate of supporting our rural economy and I have seen many successful businesses operate in rural areas, you do need to consider your business location in relation to distribution costs to ensure you are price competitive with those in your market that operate closer to transport hubs. Figure 5.16 sets out your usual order of leadership dominance.

Figure 5.16

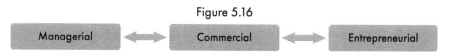

This is how you are naturally most comfortable in your leadership functions. It is important to appreciate that you need to work on achieving a balanced trio in order to lead your business effectively.

TIPS AND IDEAS

Managerial

1. Like many of the other Executive Identities, you need to develop a working three-year business plan for the business with an associated one-year operating plan. It is important to review and revise yearly.

2. You may want to consider engaging an external mentor to assist you in developing your business plan and making sure it is challenging but realistic.
3. Get involved in the recruitment of new staff and put a performance review system in place for staff with target setting and associated training.

Commercial

1. Spend time looking at the workflow in your business and make changes to improve it.
2. Understand how to read a set of accounts and how the information can inform your business decisions around buying, operational costs and capital expenditure.
3. Put a monthly management accounting system in place and use it.
4. Continually review your customers' needs and aim to meet their demands.
5. Undertake the exercise set out below to examine the appropriateness of your premises.

Entrepreneurial

1. Create specific 'ideation' thinking time in your business where all ideas are gathered and discussed. This should be ring-fenced to avoid it always seeping into day-to-day business to the point where other functions are ignored.

EXERCISE

The following is designed to assist you with an important aspect of your commercial function – the suitability of your premises. Complete the following questionnaire and highlight the changes that need to be made.

Question	Y/N	What Change Is Required?
Do you work from home?		
Do you have dedicated business premises?		
Do you own your business property?		
Do you lease your business property?		
What are your long-term commitments to the property?		
How modern are your premises?		
What are the disadvantages of your current location? Consider: site, distribution, access, facilities		

Do you need your own production facilities, or could you outsource any of the manufacturing process?		
What is the production capacity in relation to forecasted demand in your business plan?		
Will you need any investment in premises in the next three years? If so, how much?		

THE GAME CHANGER

Figure 5.17 outlines the typical imbalance that exists in the Game Changer when it comes to the trio of leadership functions.

As a Game Changer your entrepreneurial function of innovation and risk-taking as well as your passion to get your message out there through marketing in the commercial function, means these two functions dominate your trio. I have often worked with Game Changers and remark that you often need a 'chief of staff' to sweep up behind you to implement the decisions you make. As a business leader comfortable with a dominant marketing approach, you

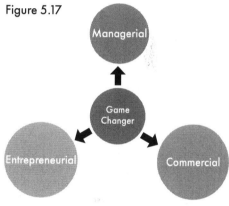

Figure 5.17

need to be able to afford a senior management team or you need to engage the other functions in your own business leadership rather quickly. In your keenness to get your message out there through your brand recognition, you often dismiss the 'more mundane' functions of the business involving people, finance, production and planning. This is how you are naturally most comfortable in your leadership functions. It is important to appreciate that you need to also have a business that is running successfully and bringing in revenue so that your message can be heard. Like the other Executive Identities, you need to work on achieving a balanced trio in order to lead your business effectively. Figure 5.18 sets out your usual order of leadership dominance.

Figure 5.18

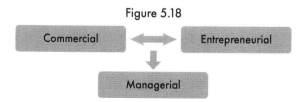

You also tend to grossly overspend on marketing and branding. The cost of the promotion of your product is something that almost every business leader underestimates. This is particularly true as you are trying to establish a new brand. The one thing you don't want to do in business is run out of money at a crucial point in your promotional campaign. Careful financial projections are the key to keeping this obstacle under control.

The saying 'perception is 9/10s of the law' has never been more relevant than it is today. We live in a world where perception and reputation seem to overshadow reality, and we just need to look at social media (or perhaps 'unsocial' media) and the lengths many will go to to protect and control their online reputation. The idea of a celebrity blogger putting a photograph online without some sort of digital enhancement is almost unheard of. Yet our teenagers take this as the truth, and it is a well-known fact that some develop eating disorders trying to keep up with the images they see.

There is no doubt that social media has provided a low-cost or even no-cost form of advertising that can propel an individual or a business onto the world stage instantly. Goggle, Amazon and Facebook all seem to have succeeded well through their online profile. However, the revolution of social media means that just about anyone can comment on your product or service within seconds, and have a worldwide audience that in turn also has an opinion. The fear of what people may say about your product or service on social media can be a real concern for you.

There has been a change in mood over the past number of years when it comes to customer care. During the 80s and 90s we were all focused on 'the customer is always right'. In recent years the business leadership thinking has moved from 'the customer is always right' to 'the customer has the right to be heard'. As a business leader it is important to instil a culture of listening to our customers, rather than letting the fear of customer dissatisfaction hold you back. This has worked well for the medical sector, where the percentage of patients taking legal cases against a hospital is significantly reduced when the medical staff apologises to patients for any errors made at the time they are made. The important lesson from this example is not to let the fear of customer dissatisfaction hold you back, but rather listen to your customers and get a reputation for quick and effective responses to their issues.

Although now an inevitable part of leading a successful business, I want to provide a note of caution. The flip side of a social media profile is the demand that your business needs to become more transparent – for example, publicly asking for feedback from your customers on social media means you are also addressing any criticisms publicly. The concept of reputation management – where individuals or companies aim to control public opinion of them or their products – is gaining revolutionary momentum. By opening up the business in this way, you need to be prepared for the continuous demand that a 24/7 presence brings, and you need to have systems, procedures and people in place to respond in a 'just in time' approach, i.e. more or less immediately. Just look at the social media revolution we have witnessed in a matter of months since the start of the Covid-19 pandemic.

Case in Point

In the late 1980s Fairtrade (whereby Fairtrade was an institutional arrangement designed to help producers in developing countries achieve better trading conditions) coffee was becoming a growing choice for consumers. I was working with a local coffee roaster who was passionate about increasing the purchase of Fairtrade products from her trade customers. The products were slightly more expensive and the retail coffee industry, although on the increase, hadn't reached any real level of consumer awareness for Fairtrade. To try to encourage increased purchases from her trade buyers the producer reduced the number and quantity of non-Fairtrade products from her trade list. Given the lacklustre consumer interest, the trade buyers simply reduced the level and quantity of orders from my coffee roaster. This particular business leader really missed the point that you need consumer buy-in as well as producer passion to make a game-changing business. By altering the trade list to its original format, some damage limitation was possible, but it took quite some time to regain the previous buying position with some of her trade customers.

TIPS AND IDEAS

Managerial

1. Ensure you operate monthly management meetings in the business and ensure everyone is working to the same targets.
2. Make sure you spend time understanding the roles and responsibilities of all the staff.
3. Engage with an external significant other sounding board who is not a Game Changer, maybe a Lifer or a Dabbler, to assist you to keep focused.

Commercial

1. Develop three-year detailed financials for the business and review expenditure against budget on a quarterly basis.
2. Focus on reviewing and controlling the marketing expenditure in your business on a monthly basis.

Entrepreneurial

1. Take time out to thoroughly examine your strategic problems before making rash strategic decisions. Research, gather information, analyse, take advice and only then make key decisions.

EXERCISE

Figure 5.19 is designed to assist you with an important aspect of your commercial function – understanding the breakeven point of your business, i.e. the income you need to earn just to cover all your overheads and cost of sales. Any income you earn over and above the breakeven point is your profit.

Figure 5.19: Business Breakeven Point

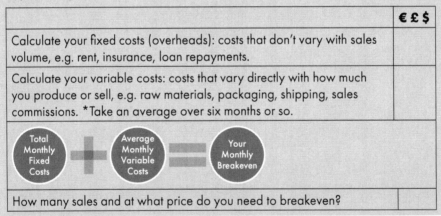

The following breakeven point is broken down to examine monthly income and expenditure. This is easy to manage and means that you can have a tighter control on your budgets.

	€ £ $
Calculate your fixed costs (overheads): costs that don't vary with sales volume, e.g. rent, insurance, loan repayments.	
Calculate your variable costs: costs that vary directly with how much you produce or sell, e.g. raw materials, packaging, shipping, sales commissions. *Take an average over six months or so.	
Total Monthly Fixed Costs ➕ Average Monthly Variable Costs ＝ Your Monthly Breakeven	
How many sales and at what price do you need to breakeven?	

SUMMARY EXERCISE

The following exercise asks that you examine the actions you need to take to try to strike a balance in your leadership functions and who might be able to help you in the process.

Executive Identity	Common Trio of Functions	Actions required to create a balance	Others who might help
Blue-Skyer			
Descendant			

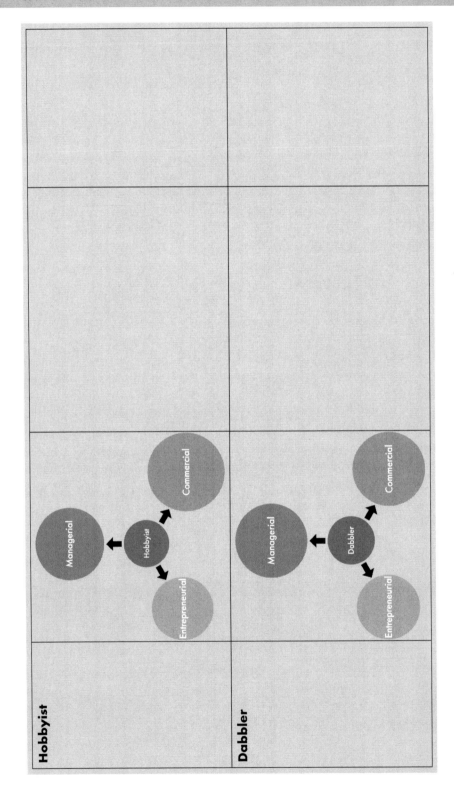

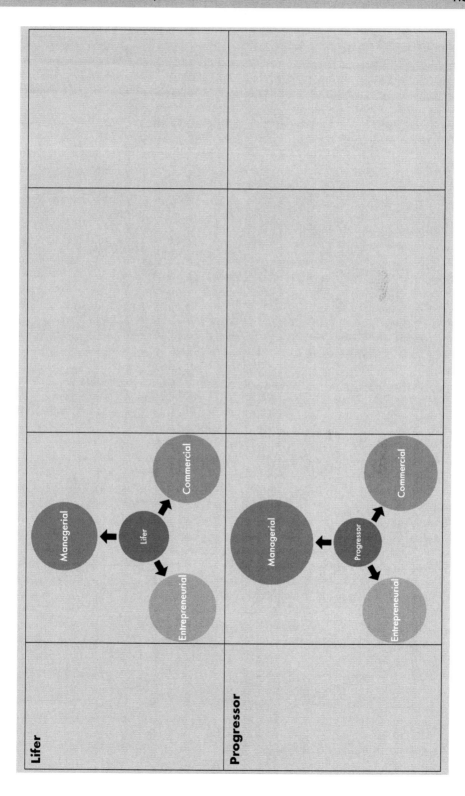

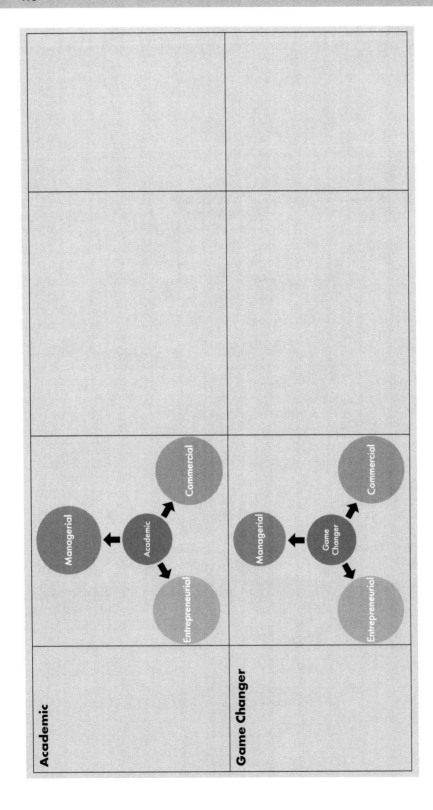

IN SUMMARY

This chapter has placed a spotlight on how your Executive Identity is directly linked to how you perform in your leadership functions in business. I have summarised these functions into three main areas I have named your Trio of Functions. Your Executive Identity will dictate the emphasis you will naturally place on each of the leadership functions, whereby you will tend to have more dominant and subservient functions. The key is always to try to strike a balance of functions in your role. If there are times you cannot do that, then at least include the skills and knowledge of others in your business to try to strike a balance.

6

MAXIMISING YOUR EFFORT

'Your living is determined not so much by what life brings to you as by the attitude you bring to life; not so much by what happens to you as by the way your mind looks at what happens.'

Khalil Gibran, poet (1883–1931)

KEY CHAPTER POINTS

✓ You can achieve maximum results by managing your effort.
✓ It is important to maximise your functional management.
✓ There is a difference between business risk and innovation risk.
✓ Each Executive Identity will have a different tolerance for risk.
✓ Good decisions can reduce business risk.

It is not always easy to understand how some people seem to succeed with such little effort. I'm sure you can easily remember the student in Maths class who seemed to do no study whatsoever and always came out with the best results. The lucky cool kid, who just didn't seem to need to study.

Through the years I have met a great number of business leaders who have discussed the importance of luck in business. Does it exist? What does it look like? When I explore a little further, many will comment about whether or not they are in the right place at the right time or the right business at the right time. There is certainly a school of business leadership that will give the idea of potluck some consideration, but most fall into the mantra that business leaders create their own luck. In fact, the idea of creating your own luck in business has been researched by Jim Collins and Morten Hansen,[11] authors of *Great by Choice: Uncertainty, Chaos, and Luck—Why Some Thrive Despite Them All*. They coined the phrase 'return on luck' (ROL) and in examining success in business their research showed that no one business has any more luck than another, but those that went on to be successful were led by business leaders who understood how to capitalise on their situations.

We can easily make the mistake that all causes in a situation or task will have the same impact on the results. To explain this a little further, I am going to call on the Pareto Principle.[12] An Italian economist, Vilfredo Pareto, first came up with the Pareto Principle, better known as the 80/20 Rule (illustrated in Figure 6.1), in 1896. In summary, Pareto stated that only a small amount of your effort (20 per cent) gives you most of your results (80 per cent).

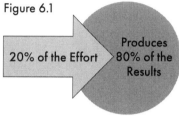

Figure 6.1

20% of the Effort → Produces 80% of the Results

Since it was first discussed the Pareto Principle has gone on to be applied to many aspects of business. For example:

- ✓ 20 per cent of the activities that you do throughout the day are responsible for 80 per cent of the results.
- ✓ 20 per cent of your customers are responsible for 80 per cent of sales.
- ✓ 20 per cent of your goods or services are responsible for 80 per cent of your business profit.
- ✓ 20 per cent of your strategic decisions could reduce 80 per cent of your risk.

Case in Point

A common example, especially when a business is at the start-up stage or entering the decline stage, is when we give equal credibility to every customer. We assume that every customer is valuable and work hard at meeting all their demands, even though there is little or no contribution by the customer to the bottom line. I was working with a design development company a few years back. At the time the business was stagnating in terms of its income and the staff seemed to be very busy without increasing its revenue. In my first meeting with the business leader it was clear that there were certain customers placing a lot of demands on the team – looking for adaptations and changes within a contract, to the point where the contracts were not making profit. At the outset I asked the business leader to write down his top 10 customers, leaving the definition of this term to him. I then asked him to write down his top 10 paying customers, i.e. those who contribute significantly to the revenue of the business and pay on time. Finally, I asked him to write down his top 10 most demanding customers, those that continually place demands on staff time for changes and adaptations. Not surprisingly, there were differences in the three lists. We then picked the top paying, less demanding customers as the key clients for the business and developed an action plan to increase the care, attention and nurturing of these customers, and to let go of the non-payers and non-contributors. The team was no longer 'busy fools'.

The aim of this chapter is to highlight how you can propel your business forward through maximising the results of your Executive Identity.

MAXIMISING YOUR FUNCTIONAL MANAGEMENT

As a business leader the Pareto Principle provides a valuable way to manage your functional strengths and to focus on the leadership tasks that make up your 20 per cent, to provide you with 80 per cent of your results. These are the tasks that you can focus on during the day and give your top priority. The implications of the Pareto Principle are sobering and should encourage you to focus on the leadership qualities that might make up your 80 per cent and your 20 per cent according to your Executive Identity. Figure 6.2 provides some suggestions to assist you to get the most out of your efforts – just like that cool kid in class who just happened to understand the Pareto Principle and get the effort and impact just right, making their own luck!

Figure 6.2: Maximising Your Functional Management

The Blue-Skyer: Maximising Your 20 Per Cent

As the Blue-Skyer you are more aligned to the entrepreneurial function, so it is a good move to surround yourself with a skilled team of managers representing the commercial and managerial functions to compensate for those areas where you are not so focused. The team can be in-house or outsourced or a combination of both. Managers with skills in planning, coordinating, production processes, financial management, distribution and marketing will be particularly useful to you. You are most likely to pay attention to the detail of any task. The positive side to this means the results are likely to be precise and deal with the problem at hand. The downside is that you can procrastinate on the 80 per cent towards the end. In other words, you are reluctant to complete as the result is never perfect in your opinion. Work with others to maintain a balanced perspective throughout and have a significant other whom you trust to push you to complete, such as your investor, business advisor or a senior member of your team.

The Descendant: Maximising Your 20 Per Cent

As the Descendant you are less aligned to the entrepreneurial function than the commercial and managerial. The culture in a family business has been developed over a number of years and sometimes tasks can become over-analysed by too many and get protracted. Hence you are most likely to involve a number of others when you make decisions and although this can be very useful for key strategic problems, it is not always appropriate for some of the day-to-day commercial or managerial decisions. It would be helpful for you to make a distinction from the outset regarding the importance of the task at hand. Perhaps get accustomed to only involving the minimum core of opinions in the less strategic tasks and get team members accustomed to this approach. Prioritising your tasks against the benefits on a day-to-day basis will enable you to make better use of your leadership skills. When you make a daily to-do list it will help to then highlight 80 per cent from that list that you do not need to do yourself and delegate those tasks to others.

The Hobbyist: Maximising Your 20 Per Cent

As the Hobbyist your commercial function is usually much stronger than your managerial and entrepreneurial functions. Your 'go-to' position for tasks is to focus on the production of your product and given that you mostly operate a small enterprise, there are few others to keep you in check. It may work well for you to make a daily to-do list of tasks and then review the list. It is likely that 80 per cent of the tasks you undertake in any one day are related to production of your product. Your Executive Identity means you need to be very disciplined in checking yourself and how you are using your time. Importantly, you need to ensure you are not putting off necessary tasks that you don't want to do, for example your tax returns, then compensating for this by spending too much time on production. As you are also close to your customers, you can suffer from giving too much attention to the poorer-paying and over-demanding customer.

The Dabbler: Maximising Your 20 Per Cent

As the Dabbler you are more aligned to the managerial and commercial functions, with a tendency to take less risk than some of the other Executive Identities. It is useful to surround yourself with innovators to assist you in examining your tasks from different perspectives. As the Dabbler you need to be mindful of not meddling too much with others working on the commercial and managerial functions in the business. Your desire to get involved in the 80 per cent means you can be busy but not always in achieving results. Your leadership needs to include the strategic direction of the business and so a good discipline for you is to consider your attitude more than your skills by learning to let go. You could examine your daily to-do list and check how many of your tasks involve overseeing others' work and try to move back and trust others to get on with their job.

The Lifer: Maximising Your 20 Per Cent

As the Lifer you usually have a balanced approach to the managerial, commercial and entrepreneurial functions. As a business leader comfortable with strategy, you can become more hands-off as the business matures. It is likely your business will get to a point in the business life cycle where your networking abilities will become very important in generating and maintaining the income into the business. In your daily to-do list it is vital that you understand the importance of your networking function and view it as an integral part of your 20 per cent rather than something that needs to be rushed through and then 'got out of the way' to move onto 'more important tasks'. Interestingly, senior managers don't always see the value of networking, but can be dismissive and even destructive. You can resolve this problem through good communication on the results you achieve through your networking role, so that they see the direct link between your role and an increase in revenue.

The Progressor: Maximising Your 20 Per Cent

As the Progressor, your managerial function tends to be your most practised. Comfortable with managing people, this will take precedence over your commercial and entrepreneurial functions. In your day-to-day leadership in the business, you may tend to get over-involved in the team and can get side-tracked easily into the 80 per cent. It is important you evaluate your daily to-do list when it is put together and ensure that the commercial and entrepreneurial functions are well represented in your 20 per cent; otherwise this neglect could cost the business dearly. You are irreplaceable in forming the strategic direction of the business, but you are really not required to undertake the ordering or staff rotas. In fact, these are just distractions you are more comfortable doing than those you need to do. Work closely with your team and give them more responsibility for the 80 per cent you need to try to offload from your to-do list. Work with your investors or business advisors to examine ways to develop your strategic direction.

The Academic: Maximising Your 20 Per Cent

As the Academic your greatest comfort zone is in innovation, with a need to work on all the other tasks that a business requires. Your daily to-do list will need to have tasks related to the managerial and commercial functions. As an Academic, you may not have asked for the business element and want to focus on the commercialisation of your product. Others, however, will look to you to set the vision, not just for the product but for the business. As you gather a team around you, it is important to prioritise skills in your senior managers that focus on the managerial and commercial functions. This way, as the business progresses it is likely you will be supported in your tasks by others. It may also be useful to bring in another researcher to the business who will relieve you of the product development tasks and give you time for the business leadership tasks. This could be a temporary position, full-time position or a function that is outsourced temporarily.

The Game Changer: Maximising Your 20 Per Cent

As the Game Changer your commercial and entrepreneurial functions tend to be more apparent than your managerial function. As such your daily to-do list can be dominated by product development and marketing. The interesting fact is that in order for you to make an impact with consumers on your 'cause', you actually need to make the whole business succeed. It might be useful for you to examine your daily list for the balance of tasks and take a ruthless approach to sieving out the 80 per cent that will not achieve results. As with the other Executive Identities, your team will look to you for overall vision and so you have a need to prioritise planning, directing, finance and production as part of your tasks. Without some of the focus of your 20 per cent on these issues, business results could be hampered or at best delayed.

TIPS AND IDEAS

The 80 per cent of the tasks you are undertaking that are responsible for just 20 per cent of the results can be delegated or outsourced to a professional who has the time and skill set to complete them successfully. Outsourcing the 80 per cent of the activities that don't produce the majority of results will allow you to focus your time and energy on completing those tasks that will help you grow your business and increase your profits.

MAXIMISING DECISION-MAKING AND REDUCING RISK

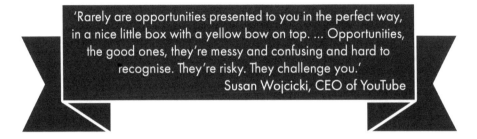

'Rarely are opportunities presented to you in the perfect way, in a nice little box with a yellow bow on top. ... Opportunities, the good ones, they're messy and confusing and hard to recognise. They're risky. They challenge you.'

Susan Wojcicki, CEO of YouTube

In the West we generally live in a culture where risk-taking is instilled as a negative trait from an early age. We all remember our parents and teachers with the mantra 'oh no, you must not do that' or 'that might not work out for you and then where will you be?' To a certain degree their caution was grounded and mainly because they cared, as with risk can come disappointment and your guardians didn't want you to get hurt. There are a few exceptions, such as 17-year-old Mohammed Islam, who came to our attention in 2014.

Mohammad started pottering in penny stocks at the age of nine and continued to trade stocks in his lunch break at New York's Stuyvesant High School. At that time, he had made eight figures trading – rumoured to be as much as $72 million.

As it is, risk is a part of life for all of us and there are certainly those who are more comfortable with it than others, maybe because of their life experiences.

Business risk is basically any situation in your leadership where there is some exposure to danger and it usually sits on a spectrum from low risk to very high risk. Like many aspects of leading a successful business, taking risks is an integral part of the process. It would be difficult to be a doctor if you always fainted at the sight of blood, and so it is with business leadership. It is almost impossible to make gains in business leadership without taking on some level of risk. For all the risks outlined in this chapter the possibility of some of the huge rewards that are possible in business is one of the key motivators for any business leader. Take Zipcar as an example – the American car-sharing company offering consumers car hire on an hourly, daily or weekly basis through a monthly membership. Started by Antje Danielson and Robin Chase, who had no experience in the sector, the company increased its initial risk investment by 6547 per cent in 13 years from 2000 to 2013. If you are uncomfortable with risk, then it is difficult to understand how you could succeed in business.

The type and scale of the risk in business leadership is, however, varied and you can be more comfortable with some types of risk over others. This is generally because there are certain risks that you expect to go hand-in-hand with business leadership. There are two that are important in considering your Executive Identity:

1. General business risk – this can cover new markets, new audiences, and new capabilities. It will encourage you to take steps towards future success. Many people

can give into the little voices that say 'this isn't the right time or the right place' and as a business leader you need to learn to move past this.

2. Innovation risk – supporting creativity and innovation in your business means you are indirectly giving a nod to risk. It can infiltrate across all the leadership functions, including managerial, commercial and entrepreneurial. For example, in the entrepreneurial function you should expect regular failures in product design in the quest to hit on the one that works.

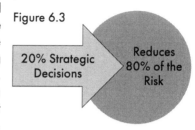

Figure 6.3

20% Strategic Decisions

Reduces 80% of the Risk

In fact, much business theory focuses on the fact that innovation creates its own level of risk – having high risk with low impact at the beginning of the innovation process and moving to lower risk and high impact before the product is launched to the market.

Figure 6.4: General Business Risk

Low / High

Hobbyist Academic

Blue-Skyer Lifer Game Changer

Descendant Dabbler Progressor

Medium

As a business leader you are making decisions on a constant basis, from the mundane to the strategic and anything in between. The time you devote to a particular problem should depend on the risk involved and its size, complexity and impact. Some decisions will have minimum risk and require minimal investment, while others could be catastrophic and require significant investment with high risks. The ability to make effective, timely decisions and reduce risk as much as possible is a fundamental business leadership quality.

We can legitimately apply the Pareto Principle to decisions, concluding that 20 per cent of your strategic decisions should aim to reduce 80 per cent of the business risk, as shown in Figure 6.3.

This is a sobering thought and should make us consider the complexity of some of the decisions we

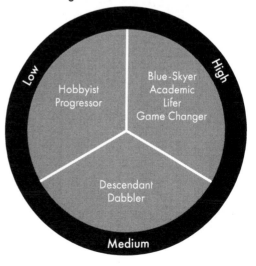

Figure 6.5: Innovation Risk

Low / High

Hobbyist Progressor

Blue-Skyer Academic Lifer Game Changer

Descendant Dabbler

Medium

make. As shown in Figures 6.4 and 6.5, each Executive Identity will have different tolerance levels to overall business risk and innovation risk and therefore different approaches are required to reduce exposure to risk.

The Blue-Skyer

Your tolerance for both strategic and innovation risk is high as you are engaged with it so much, particularly at the start-up and reinvention stage. Your business requires intense resources and you are breaking new ground with new product development with no real confirmation in the marketplace as to whether it will work or not. As a business leader you are continually working to deadlines. These can be product launches, tender deadlines for new contracts, delivery timelines for contract completion and so on. The risk of delays on deadlines can have significant negative financial impacts on already strained finances. This could be penalties for not completing projects on time – common in the construction sector – or delayed product launches leading to overstretching cash flows and the patience of investors. This makes the business and the product development risky and something you have come to learn to live with.

Defining the problem correctly (Figure 6.6) will save a lot of time, energy and money later. Poorly defined problems have a habit of leading to poor decisions. So, you need to look at the problem very closely and get a clear picture of what is happening. Working with others to get a different perspective is invaluable, as is breaking the problem down into smaller pieces to get a clearer point of view, much like the segments of a wheel of cheese.

Figure 6.6

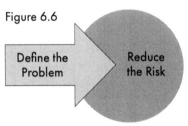

Define the Problem → Reduce the Risk

TIPS AND IDEAS

1. There are some key questions you could ask about the problem at this stage, such as:
   a. How important is the issue?
   b. How many people are involved?
   c. Could it get worse with no attention?
   d. What seems to be the cause of the problem?

The Descendant

Your tolerance for both strategic and innovation risk is medium as you are prepared to take some level of risk on both, but high-risk strategies don't tend to sit well with you. Your family has spent a long time building up the business and you are likely to feel the responsibility of your decisions. When you launch a new product or reinvent the business you will of course run your projections and make the risks you take as calculated as can possibly be. The real interest, however, in your business or product is still an unknown. Consumers can be fickle and you really have no idea of the reality of the popularity of what you have done, until it is out there in the marketplace with all the resources already invested. If your projections are off, then it could be difficult for the business to recover.

You are unlikely to want to risk the business too much, but appreciate business growth requires some level of risk. You therefore need to gather information and appreciate where the information is coming from and why it is being provided (Figure 6.7). This part of decision-making can sometimes be the trickiest and the one that can lead you to the poorer solution. Your options for sources of information are endless and can include:

Figure 6.7

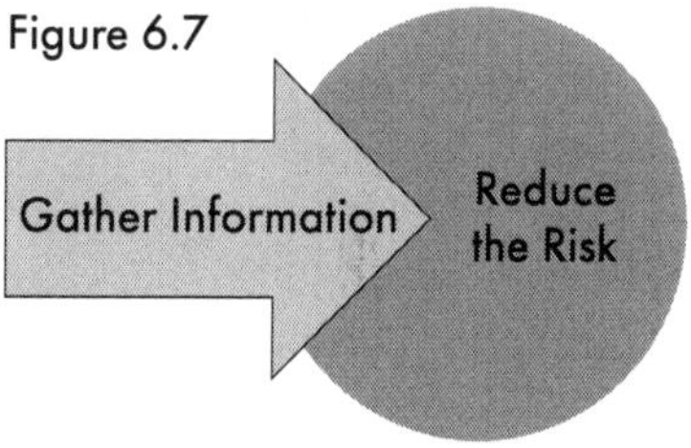

- ✓ Theoretical research
- ✓ Written reports
- ✓ Members of your board of directors
- ✓ Staff from senior management, operations, department heads and frontline staff
- ✓ Customers
- ✓ Suppliers
- ✓ Financers
- ✓ Professional advisors

I am sure you are well aware that in business leadership there are many around you who have a vested interest in one solution to a problem over another and so you need to gather information from as many sources, with as many viewpoints and from as many people as possible within your timeframe.

The Hobbyist

Your tolerance for strategic business risk and innovation risk is generally low. This is mainly because you have very limited resources to take any risk either with employment or financially. You are likely to have invested some personal capital or capital security into the business, perhaps more than once, putting your financial risk-taking right up there. It is unlikely that any business can rely solely on external funding throughout the business lifecycle and so you have to delve into your savings, bank accounts or house security to get things started or to keep things going. By doing so you could be forfeiting or at least decreasing your safety net. Without the tangible support of others, you may believe any further risk is just not open to you. Unfortunately, this can be a vicious circle, as without growth the unavailability of resources will continue in the long term, relegating you to the sole trader bracket, and this is not always the way you want your business to progress. The difficulty I have also seen with this is the guilt that Hobbyists can feel when they have depleted the funds for their children's university education or their first house, and as yet the business has not returned what it should.

The Dabbler

Your tolerance for both strategic and innovation risk is medium. You have an appreciation that to be in business at all you need to take some risks, and equally if you are an investor in another business. However, you are generally uncomfortable with too much risk to your hard-earned funds. As the Dabbler you need to examine your options (Figure 6.8) to make your decisions.

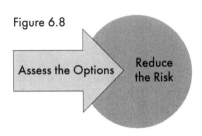

Figure 6.8

Assess the Options   Reduce the Risk

Here I am going to borrow some analogies from the work of economists and economic appraisals. When an economist carries out an economic appraisal on a capital expenditure, they will examine a number of options and cost these options in both financial and non-financial terms to come up with the Best VFM (Value for Money) solution to address the problem. So for example the problem could be the lack of classroom space in a school and the economist needs to look at various options, including sharing classroom space with another school, keeping the number of entrants to the school in line with current capacity or, indeed, a new build of classrooms. The important message I want to borrow is that the option analysis has a habit of following the same set structure:

✓ Option 1 – Do nothing
✓ Option 2 – Maintain the status quo
✓ Option 3 – Solution A
✓ Option 4 – Solution B
✓ Option 5 – Solution C

It is important to examine all the options and critically look at the benefits and costs of each. A decision is really providing a solution to a problem and the difference between good and poor decisions really comes down to how much we understand the problem and put our solution in place. When we make a decision, we are really choosing a solution from a selection of options. You need to evaluate all the alternatives and the best solution may not always be the cheapest or the easiest or the quickest. You could also be limited on time and only a few options will meet the deadline. The interesting thing about this approach is to always remember that doing nothing and maintaining the status quo are options that should always be part of your decision-making process. Decisions do not always require change and in fact some of the best decisions in business can be to maintain the status quo.

Case in Point

One of the most common problems that hits any expanding business is what to do about the increasing need for production facilities. In many cases this is driven by the promise of new orders from existing or new customers. In my experience from working with business leaders the natural go-to solution is usually to expand production capability through building on to the existing premises or moving to bigger premises. It is a difficult decision with many implications, and most importantly an increase in immediate capital costs, as well as an increase in ongoing operational costs of running new equipment and paying additional staff. All on the basis that new orders will be forthcoming.

It is a risky time in any business and I have spent many hours assisting business leaders to examine alternative solutions, especially short-term solutions to assess the longer-term commitment of the new customers to new contracts. These can often include options to outsource additional production or to take storage pre- or post-production off-site to allow for further production capacity on-site. In a number of cases, the temporary solution was enough and became the long-term permanent solution. This is a much cheaper and less disruptive way forward than building new premises or a relocation of premises.

The Lifer

Your tolerance for both strategic business risk and innovation risk tends to be high. You are accustomed to taking numerous risks with both before hitting on that successful business idea. You tend to take the approach that you cannot let risk hold you back – you are in business and it shouldn't steer you away from pursuing your goals. Having probably tried a few business ideas that were unsuccessful you have become a little immune to risk and see it as part of getting to the successful growing business.

Having a plan of activities (Figure 6.9) will assist you in reducing your risk. This plan is important and should make clear to all those involved what needs to be done, by whom and when. Communicating your decision is important for making sure it is accepted and that everyone who is required buys into the solution. It is not unusual where you have a team of senior managers and a complex solution that you will need to spend time selling and communicating the solution. This can make the difference between a successful solution and a solution without traction.

Figure 6.9

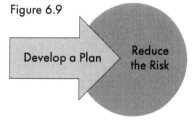

Develop a Plan → Reduce the Risk

The Progressor

Your tolerance for strategic business risk is medium and tends to be more than your tolerance for innovation risk, which sits on low. As a business leader you tend to accept that there will be some business risk in creating a strong lifestyle business. There are many distinctions between an employee and a business leader, but the one that seems to attract the most attention is the fact that you have abandoned the option to have a steady monthly salary. I'm not sure that you are as comfortable with this scenario as others may think, but the reality is you have given up the option and the pressure is on to create your lifestyle again as quickly as possible. It is vital that your business brings you in an income from very early on, but there is no certainty that this will happen.

Apart from strategic risk, you often view innovation as a high-risk approach, and in your book, you tend to take the attitude 'if it ain't broke then don't fix it!' Innovation does not tend to be high on your agenda. Continuous evaluation of your targets (Figure 6.10) will enable you learn for future leadership decisions.

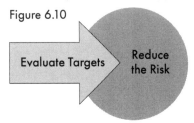

Figure 6.10

The Academic

Your Executive Identity is unique when it comes to risk as you have tolerance levels that are usually at opposite ends of the spectrum. Although your tolerance for business strategic risk can be low, your tolerance for innovation risk is high. There are probably no surprises here for you, as your reduced practical business acumen can mean that you don't fully appreciate some of the strategic risks that are required to grow your R&D into a sustainable, growing empire. Your ability to tolerate innovation risk is, however, well-developed and used on a fairly continuous and daily basis. Taking calculated decisions (Figure 6.11) is crucial to assisting your business to grow.

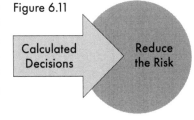

Figure 6.11

Calculated decisions involve effective risk management and then taking the jump. Understanding it is important not to over-analyse risks, you should do your due diligence by examining every strategic project with a risk management plan that outlines contingencies to negate any major risks. The world of theatre has been managing major risks for centuries by ensuring there is an understudy for all the key parts in a show. The understudy is someone who knows all the lines and could take over from the main actors if something happened and they were unable to perform on a particular evening.

The Game Changer

Your tolerance for risk is high as you are trying to increase consumer awareness in a particular issue and basing a business on that issue. This is always a risky venture with many obstacles along the way and you can become very tolerant at trying to look at different ways to get your message across. You do appreciate that each risk decision you make usually carries some degree of costs in time and money, and accept this as part of the journey to assist consumers to become educated and buy into your message. To reduce your risk, you can take each of your strategic decisions around the decision-making cycle, illustrated in Figure 6.12.

Figure 6.12

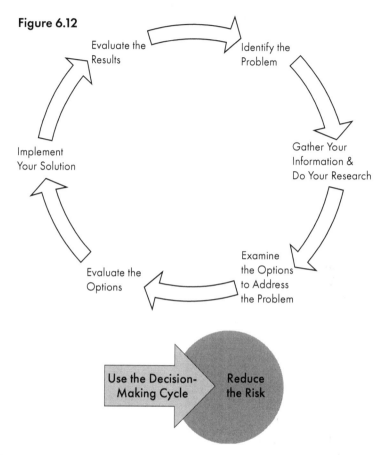

RISK MANAGEMENT

For all the projects that could create a medium to high risk in your business, it's a good idea to put a risk register in place that you can continually refer to and work on. This doesn't need to be complicated, it just needs to be realistic and there are six basic steps to create your register as set out in Figure 6.13.

In the first instance you will need to identify the risks in the project – you cannot resolve a risk if you don't know what it is in the first place. It is useful to talk with as many relevant people

Figure 6.13

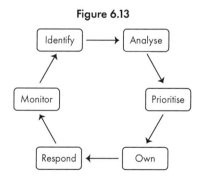

as possible to get as many perspectives as possible. This is perhaps a good time to include the 'glass is always half-empty' person in the business. Their negative outlook will enable you to see the risks that you or others may miss.

Once you have your list of risks, then it's time to determine how likely each of the risks are to happen. This could be as simple as not very likely to most likely. When this is done you will need to prioritise, and it could simply be categorising each risk into high, medium and low. Some risks are going to require immediate attention as they could derail your project while others are much less threatening.

You now need someone to watch out for the risk and deal with resolving it when and if required. Importantly, as far as possible, this should not be you. You have a lot to do in leading a business, so monitoring several risks as well means some balls are going to get dropped. Whoever you assign, just make sure they have the experience and skills needed. If in fact the risk should then occur, you need to put your contingencies in place and mitigate any loss. It's important that the owner of the risk then monitors its resolution and reports back to you on a regular basis.

TIPS AND IDEAS

1. There is a fine line between good risk (or calculated risk) and bad risk. Understanding the difference between the two can mean the difference between wise business decisions and careless mistakes. Calculated risk, as the title suggests, is about careful project planning, while bad risk tends to be a result of haste and thoughtlessness. The fact that we have many successful business leaders who would not have arrived at their current position without taking calculated risks is evidence that it can be done.
2. Identify your understudy in your business. Take time to think about who it is, or who it could be, with some training and mentoring.

SUMMARY EXERCISE

The following provides a template you can use to create your own risk register.

Project Title			
Possible Risks			
Probability of Occurrence Most Unlikely = 1 Most Likely = 5			
Category of Risk (High, Medium, Low)			
Person Managing Risk			
Planned Response if Risk Occurs			
Frequency of Risk Monitoring			

The risks that score 3 or more for probability of occurrence and medium-to-high for category of risk are those that should get the most attention from you as the business leader.

In Summary

For some Executive Identities, decision-making can come easier than to others and no doubt it is an ability that improves with practice – as the saying goes, 'practice makes perfect'. The following provides a summary of the approach to decision-making we discussed throughout the chapter.

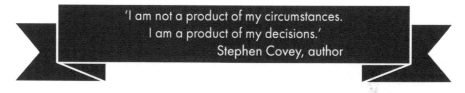

'I am not a product of my circumstances.
I am a product of my decisions.'
Stephen Covey, author

Executive Identity	Your Summary Approach to Decision-Making
Blue-Skyer	You are continuously dealing with invention problems and can use this to improve your overall business leadership decision-making. Your greatest challenge is not to rush in with a decision before you have fully assessed the problem and the options available.
Descendant	You are likely to get plenty of chances to practice your decision-making skills as you lead a business that has been operating for a number of years with a team of staff. Problems can become over-analysed as there are too many points of view from too many people. For this reason, making a decision can take longer than it really should do.
Hobbyist	Of all the Executive Identities you are the most likely to have to recognise a problem and solve it on your own. Hopefully you engage your external sounding boards to support you. You may not always see the problem, or you may see it but are reluctant to make a decision, especially if it's not directly related to the product or sale of your products.
Dabbler	You will have been involved in many decisions and can use this to your advantage. However, you can have a casual approach to decision-making – not always seeing it as an important part of your business leadership.

Lifer	You have a way of sieving out the importance of problems and prioritising their significance. You tend to involve others in the decision-making process; however you can tend to delegate decisions without checking out the ability of the team member to implement solutions.
Progressor	You can be very positive and involve your team in your decision-making. The key is not to let the process drag out to the point of over-analysis with limited implementation of solutions.
Academic	You have plenty of experience in product problem-solving and can have a tendency to take a theoretical perspective to a problem and therefore your solutions can be blinkered without taking time to examine the practical implications of the problem.
Game Changer	You can be very creative when finding solutions to problems and can use this to your advantage. As you can also over-dissect a problem it is key that you have confidence in your solutions.

7

YOUR INTER EXECUTIVE IDENTITIES

> 'The union of opposites, in so far as they are really complementary, always results in the most perfect harmony; and the seemingly incongruous is often the most natural.'
> Stefan Zweig, *Beware of Pity* (1939)

KEY CHAPTER POINTS

- ✓ Executive Identities can be complimentary.
- ✓ Complimentary Executive Identities can be found in business partners, silent investors, your senior management team and business advisors.
- ✓ Certain Executive Identities will conflict with others in business leadership.
- ✓ Consider your Executive Identity when recruiting your team members or board of directors.
- ✓ Your Executive Identity may alter with your life career.

As a business leader, in trying to do your best you can sometimes forget that others can assist you to reach your goals – if we allow them in. It may seem you are making all the decisions, but there is likely to be at least one other key strategic person influencing your business leadership, such as a business partner, chairperson, advisor or silent investor. This expands even further if you start to gather a senior management team around you. For this reason, this chapter will focus on the co-existence of Executive Identities in different ways in business leadership.

EXECUTIVE IDENTITY PAIRING

Co-Existence

When two forces that should work together do work together a synergy is created where the whole is greater than the sum of the parts. In other words, 1+1= more than 2. This is exactly what can happen when two complimentary Executive Identities come together in business leadership. I have observed many co-existing Executive Identities providing real complementarity and added value to their business leadership. As the saying goes, 'two heads are better than one', and with two people sharing the responsibility it can ease the pressure on any one business leader. There are other very legitimate reasons for Executive Identity pairing in business leadership, including:

- ✓ You can double up on your efforts and networks to reach new customers.
- ✓ It can act as a catalyst for greater creativity and innovation in product development, and overall strategic business growth.
- ✓ You can play 'good cop, bad cop' when it comes to suppliers, employees, etc.
- ✓ Another Executive Identity can help you take greater risks or hold you back from taking too many risks.
- ✓ It's good to celebrate or cry together.

Opposites Attract

We have probably all carried out the school science experiment where we have put together two magnets with their opposing poles facing each other. Once they snap together, they are almost impossible to break apart. So it is with your Executive Identity. There is a need in business leadership to ensure you have others around you to compensate for your weaknesses and allow for the maximum experience, skills and knowledge to be brought to the business. This type of pairing can address overall business growth – including the normal business functions of marketing, finance and HR. In this pairing process there is usually a mixing of skills, knowledge and abilities in the strategic management of the business. It is important to have a pool of experience to draw on as you work your way through the business life cycle. As business leaders it can be hard for us to accept our weaknesses. However, for those who do and bring other leadership influencers around them, there are many rewards.

STRATEGIC BUSINESS PARTNERSHIPS

Over 62 per cent of all UK businesses operate as sole traders,[13] which means the business is registered under one person with a self-employed status. Appreciating that this is a high number of businesses operating as just one individual, it is, however, very rare that you as a business leader will be operating alone. In the following grid I have identified the Executive Identity that most supports and compliments your leadership with a rationale for that choice. For some business leaders, there are two Executive Identities that could equally support you and are equally suitable for the role.

Executive Identity	Rationale
Blue-Skyer — Dabbler	As the Blue-Skyer you are creative and innovative and focused on your product or service development. One of the most important elements of your business leadership is having a 'steady hand' to lead the business with you to the market. The Dabbler offers this experience and potential investment.
Academic / Descendant / Game Changer	As the Descendant you are most likely in the business when it needs to reinvent and stop any decline. For this reason the support of creative thinking based on up-to-date research through the Academic can be an attractive pairing. I also include the Game Changer as this pairing may suit both business leaders. For the Descendant a 'cause' may just be the reinvention the business needs and for the Game Changer the backing of a well-established business can be very lucrative.
Hobbyist — Dabbler	Like the Blue-Skyer, the Hobbyist is a creative business leader and sometimes needs the support of those who have contacts, networks and extensive experience. The Dabbler is a pairing that has resulted in many benefits in my experience.
Blue-Skyer / Dabbler / Academic	As the Dabbler you are looking around for somewhere to use your knowledge and networks, and hoping to come across an idea you can invest in. I suggest your hunting ground should be with high-growth business start-ups found with the Blue-Skyers and the Academics looking for a way to commercialise their research.

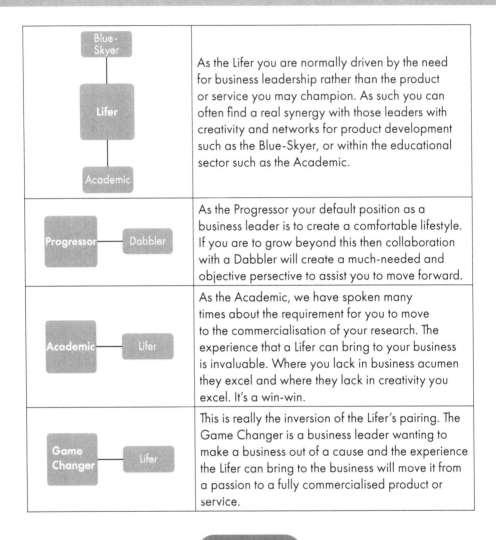

Blue-Skyer / Lifer / Academic	As the Lifer you are normally driven by the need for business leadership rather than the product or service you may champion. As such you can often find a real synergy with those leaders with creativity and networks for product development such as the Blue-Skyer, or within the educational sector such as the Academic.
Progressor — Dabbler	As the Progressor your default position as a business leader is to create a comfortable lifestyle. If you are to grow beyond this then collaboration with a Dabbler will create a much-needed and objective persective to assist you to move forward.
Academic — Lifer	As the Academic, we have spoken many times about the requirement for you to move to the commercialisation of your research. The experience that a Lifer can bring to your business is invaluable. Where you lack in business acumen they excel and where they lack in creativity you excel. It's a win-win.
Game Changer — Lifer	This is really the inversion of the Lifer's pairing. The Game Changer is a business leader wanting to make a business out of a cause and the experience the Lifer can bring to the business will move it from a passion to a fully commercialised product or service.

Case in Point

I worked very recently with a local sole trader retail business where the business leader was really struggling and needed help. The main problem was the business was tired and really not showing any green shoots of growth. In looking around the premises you could see that there had been limited or no investment into the equipment or décor for some time. I also examined the strengths and weaknesses of the current owner. He was a Progressor who had set up his own business five years previously, after leaving a job he had held for ten years because there were limited career opportunities. He was a very methodical and organised leader dealing with all the buying, stock management, staff rota, accounts and government returns. He had also surrounded himself with similar types of people. He lacked any real enthusiasm or any creative thoughts to reinvent the business. I strongly suggested that he engage in a business angel programme where he might find a silent investor in the business, such as a Dabbler, to inject some much-needed cash and new thinking to move the business forward.

TIPS AND IDEAS

Remember that complimentary Executive Identities can be introduced into your business in a variety of ways. The common denominator is that they must have a key influencing role and you must see them as a co-leader.

EXERCISE

1. Consider your Inter Executive Identity and how you can involve that person in your business at a leadership level. As a starting point consider the following roles:
   a. Partner
   b. Investor
   c. Advisor
2. Complete the following activity plan.

Inter Executive Identity	Role	Action to Engage	Completed By
		1. 2. 3. 4.	

YOUR TEAM OR BOARD OF DIRECTORS

When we discuss your business leadership in the Executive Identity Model® we also need to examine your senior management team and your possible board of directors (board). Marvel Comics first introduced us to the idea of superheroes in 1939 – these were individuals who could take on the problems of the world, single-handedly. Then in 2019 Marvel Studios released one of the highest income-generating movies of all time, by bringing all the superheroes together and creating a team. In recruiting for your team or formally establishing a board, I suggest you consider your Inter Executive Identities very carefully.

Constructive Diversity

As humans, we tend to be creatures of habit. We like to surround ourselves with those who look like us, think like us and identify with the same things that we do. When you bring together your team or your board, I suggest you stay well away from this norm unless you want a lot of 'yes' people to surround you, with little to offer by way of constructive input. It is really important to have diversity on your team or board – however it should be constructive diversity.

This is when you bring together a group of people with different perspectives to support your decision-making in your business leadership. They can be diverse in experience, backgrounds, Executive Identity and even age, to give you different perspectives and enable you to make decisions that have been analysed in different ways. This is a really constructive way to place yourself in other people's shoes and see their perspective on your decisions. This is so valuable in effective business leadership and something you are unable to achieve by yourself.

Figure 7.1 outlines the contribution each Executive Identity can provide to a team or board of directors.

Figure 7.1 Contribution of Board Members

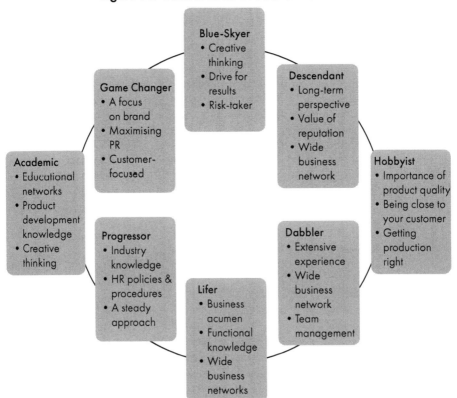

Based on the above summary of contributions by each Executive Identity, the following provides an outline of the most constructive core of Executive Identities you could have on a senior management team or board depending on your own business leadership Executive Identity.

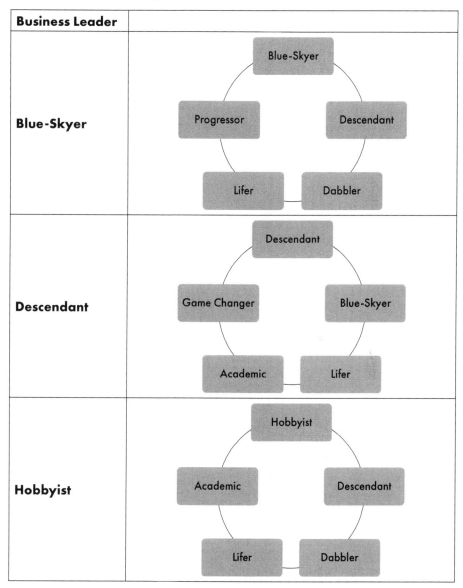

Business Leader	
Blue-Skyer	Blue-Skyer, Progressor, Descendant, Lifer, Dabbler
Descendant	Descendant, Game Changer, Blue-Skyer, Academic, Lifer
Hobbyist	Hobbyist, Academic, Descendant, Lifer, Dabbler

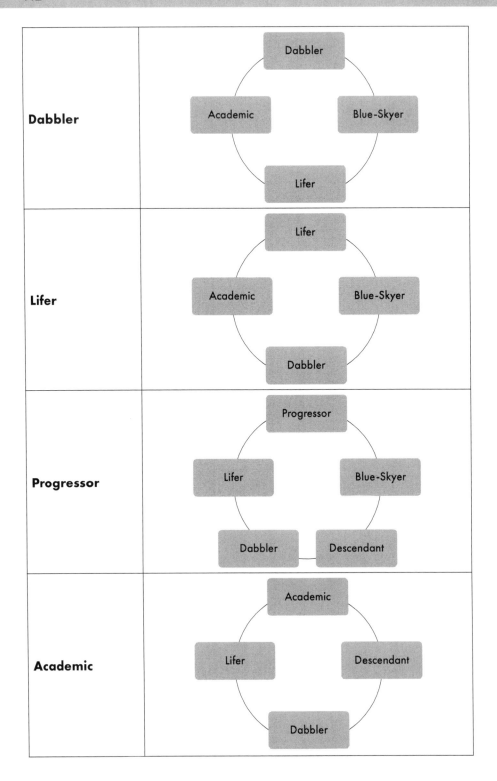

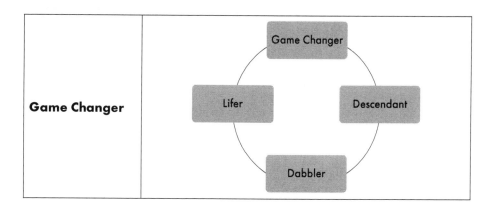

Recruiting Executive Identities

This model of core Executive Identities is most useful when you are recruiting new members to your board or team. By examining the leadership that is already around the table and meeting the gaps, you are most likely to have a winning team. When recruiting your board or team members it is important you use the interview process to assess the Executive Identities of the candidates. There is a questioning process that can assist you to delve into the Executive Identity – the case study approach.

One of the most useful ways to assess someone else's Executive Identity is to work on a case study basis. When you ask someone to describe the way they would deal with a leadership situation it can tell you a lot about their Executive Identity. The most common structure to use for the case study approach is STAR.

Situation	Let the candidate describe a situation where they had to work a leadership quality identified by you. For example, controlling financial spending, or lack of innovation in a team.
Task	Let the candidate outline what the task was within the situation. What was it they needed to do as a leader?
Action	Let the candidate describe what actions they personally took to undertake the task.
Results	What results did the candidate achieve?

For example, when asked about developing a strategic direction for an organisation a Blue-Skyer is more likely to emphasise their encouragement of new thinking to the problem, whereas the Dabbler will focus on the resource options for strategic development such as finance, people and premises.

TIPS AND IDEAS

1. Recruit your senior management team carefully as you are going to invest a lot of your time and energy into making sure they work effectively and efficiently in your business or department.
2. If at first you don't succeed, try, try and try again. Do not be tempted to recruit a senior manager who is OK – look for the best. You deserve the best and it will make life an awful lot quieter in the long run.
3. It is good to have an odd number of board members. This way you will avoid a 'hung' decision as there will always be a winning decision, even if it must rest on a majority vote being reached.
4. Make sure you invest in your board. Spend time with each board member and get their perspective on your issues both individually and collectively.

The Clash of Executive Identities

As there are Executive Identities that work well together, there are those that most definitely struggle in the same business, team, board or department. This adversity can be a competitive rivalry, or it can be when each leader's ideas, attitudes and actions are in direct opposition to each other. Like oil and water there are Executive Identities that just do not mix in leadership and limit any progress through their association. Like most things in life, in my business experience it really is best to compliment your leadership rather than waste valuable time on trying to make the square and the circle fit together! The following outlines the least complimentary leadership Executive Identity for you.

Executive Identity	Rationale
Blue-Skyer **+** Game Changer **=** Confusion	When you place two creative identities together this can be a recipe for confusion.
Descendant **+** Dabbler **=** Procrastination	There really is little added value the Dabbler could offer the Descendant. With a lack of real reinvention this relationship is most likely to lead to procrastination.
Hobbyist **+** Blue-Skyer **=** No Mutual Ground	Importantly the Hobbyist is driven by a passion for what they enjoy doing. Although the Blue-Skyer is probably leading in a similar way their objectives and ambitions are very different. Through experience I know these two Executive Identities have very little in common.

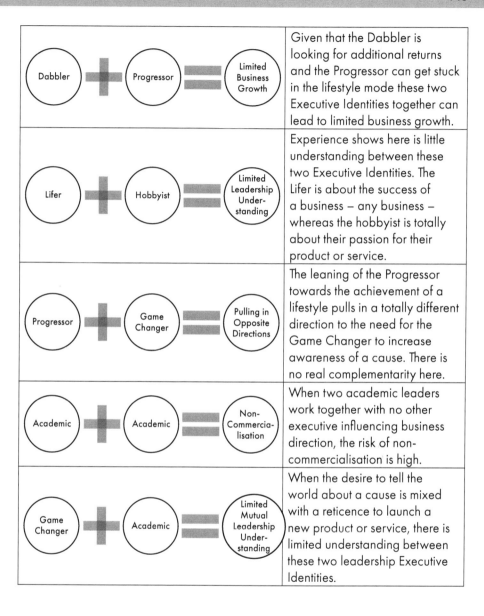

Dabbler + Progressor = Limited Business Growth	Given that the Dabbler is looking for additional returns and the Progressor can get stuck in the lifestyle mode these two Executive Identities together can lead to limited business growth.	
Lifer + Hobbyist = Limited Leadership Understanding	Experience shows here is little understanding between these two Executive Identities. The Lifer is about the success of a business – any business – whereas the hobbyist is totally about their passion for their product or service.	
Progressor + Game Changer = Pulling in Opposite Directions	The leaning of the Progressor towards the achievement of a lifestyle pulls in a totally different direction to the need for the Game Changer to increase awareness of a cause. There is no real complementarity here.	
Academic + Academic = Non-Commercialisation	When two academic leaders work together with no other executive influencing business direction, the risk of non-commercialisation is high.	
Game Changer + Academic = Limited Mutual Leadership Understanding	When the desire to tell the world about a cause is mixed with a reticence to launch a new product or service, there is limited understanding between these two leadership Executive Identities.	

SUMMARY EXERCISE

Given your Executive Identity, use the following table to identify the Executive Identities that could compliment you, your team or board of directors.

My Executive Identity	Those Executive Identities that Could Compliment My Business Leadership

IN SUMMARY

Whatever the circumstances surrounding your board and team, knowing how to link Executive Identities so they can support you to be a successful business leader needs consideration. Complimentary Inter Executive Identities can go a long way to assist you to be a successful business leader operating a successful business or department for many years. Finding the best fit for your leadership identity will enable you to maximise your impact on your business growth. Equally, it is important to be aware of those Executive Identities that are least complimentary and may only waste your time in the long run. Having a core of complimentary Executive Identities for your board of directors or senior management team will assist you in succeeding in your business leadership.

There is also the informal team that every one of us as a business leader should gather around us. These are certain people who have always been around us and they are our go-to sounding boards – the ones we automatically talk to – and we will deal with this in the next chapter.

8

YOUR SUPPORT TEAM

> 'There are emotional relationships in any business.'
> D. Tompkins, American entrepreneur (1943–2015)

KEY CHAPTER POINTS

✓ Relationships are key to business leadership.
✓ Even if there is only you, you still need a team around you to run an effective business.
✓ Entrepreneurs have a greater tendency for social isolation and need to work hard at their relationships.
✓ Being a leader in business changes relationships.
✓ It's not always the most obvious relationships that need attention.

There's nothing like becoming a business leader to change the dynamic of your relationships. All your relationships, existing and new – family, friends, old colleagues and new business peers. You will hopefully make some new friends and many colleagues along the way. Sadly, you may very likely lose one or two as well. You cannot control the attitude of others to you going into business, but you can control how you manage this time of change. The interesting aspect is that your support may come from the least expected places. Parents may be unsupportive since you could be giving up a well-paid full-time position, friends may be wary, and colleagues may be jealous that you have taken the plunge into something they hold a secret desire to do. When we look at Maslow's Hierarchy of Needs, one thing is certain, regardless of which level of need you may or may not be at on the hierarchy– each level, beyond physiological needs, demands relationships. We are about to explore some important aspects of your relationships so that you understand how to manage your new environment.

IN THE BEGINNING

I am going to work on the assumption that most people have had a job somewhere at some point in their lives outside of their own business. At the very least this could have been a Saturday or part-time job, when you were at school or a student at university. It doesn't matter where or when. What I want you to try to remember was how you felt walking into the first day of that job – what were you concerned about in this new adventure? Without too much analysis, I would take a bet that high on your agenda was who you would meet. What would they be like? How would you get along with them (or not)? Would you make any new friends? What would your boss be like?

Why, then, is this such an unimportant part of what we think about when we go into business? We seem to envisage a life alone or with a business partner, only interrupted when employees may or may not come along during business growth. We see this as the extent of the relationships we will have or, more importantly, need. I sometimes wonder if entrepreneurs taking their first foray into business think they are entering a monastery!

Setting up and leading a business can indeed seem very isolating at the start. There are a number of reasons for this, not least because you often feel the responsibility for success constantly on your shoulders. This is not a burden you may feel you can share very often with your managers, and your decisions can often affect their positions, job security, etc. The situation can be compounded further if you are in business by yourself (the solo self-employed) or working from home. Sole traders are now a vital element of the UK economy, contributing around £271 billion to the economy.[14] New research undertaken by Epson backs this up. The research, which surveyed 1,000 UK freelancers, found that 91 per cent of the solo self-employed worked from home at least some of the time. A striking 48 per cent of those surveyed admitted to finding it 'lonely' and 46 per cent said it was 'isolating'. The Blue-Skyer, Hobbyist and Academic can be particularly prone to social isolation as, certainly in the beginning, you tend to operate as sole traders. You may have moved from working alongside tutors and lecturers (Academic) or many years with work colleagues in a large organisation (Dabbler or Progressor). Whatever the circumstances, when you first go into business it can feel very lonely. What seemed like a good idea when you were commuting to work for three hours every day on packed public transport suddenly feels daunting. I say suddenly, because it is. One day you work in a large organisation with a lot of employees and a team around you, then – well – it's just you!

I have also noticed a particular issue with Lifers. Since business has always been your first career choice, you may well have gone into business at a young age, possibly between 16 and 20 years and often before too many deep friendships have been formed. If you are a Lifer, then be aware that you may have missed out on the development of lifelong friendships by not going to college, and that can leave a tremendous gap that you need to fill – and quickly!

My late mother was a very wise person in so many ways and always remarked that if you sit in the house and expect people to constantly call and visit you, then you are much mistaken. If you want relationships and support, then you are the one who needs to engage. You need to 'seek and you shall find!' I'm afraid if you're feeling isolated you only have yourself to blame. Isolation is self-inflicted! You are allowing the everyday grind of trying to sell, deal with production equipment problems, supplier issues, filling out VAT forms or even cleaning the floors to get in the way of some crucial relationship-building. It is a fact that business leaders tend towards cutting themselves off from the outside world, which is marginalising and counter-productive to leading a successful business. Of course the risk of isolation is compounded further due to the fallout from the Covid-19 pandemic. You are required to dig even deeper to ensure you keep up with your contacts and networks and much of that can be through online communication. But keep up with these you must.

There are steps you can take to try to minimise loneliness. Over the past few years we have seen a significant rise in innovation hubs, co-working spaces, hot desking and incubation units to name but a few. These are extremely low-cost options for your business and even if you believe your business can't yet afford to pay an additional cost, I would bet money on it that the increase in your productivity (and therefore revenue) after the first six months will cover the cost. It is always a difficult decision to take on an extra cost in business but looking after yourself is priceless.

Case in Point

Over the years I have heard some wonderful renditions of how entrepreneurs have ended up in business. One of my most memorable was a woman – a Progressor – I met some years ago who left a CEO position in a large charity to set up her own counselling service. She conveyed the story of when she first went into business, moving from having a team of staff with several specialities and being able to lift a phone to get IT support, HR advice or a lunchtime sandwich if someone was going to the local shop. She left her job on the Friday and started in her wonderful new business on the Monday. This consisted of a desk, a chair, a telephone and a computer in a very dark unit in her local enterprise centre. Sadly, the computer was new, and she had no idea how to get it up and running, so she went to lift the phone to call IT and realised that wasn't an option. My client goes on to explain how she sat there for a while and stared at the computer screen, with tears in her eyes, really wondering what she had done. After a couple of hours had passed, she made her way round to the reception of the enterprise centre and very quickly had contact details for at least three computer experts who could help her out. With that she realised she wasn't just on her own and that by reaching out she could survive.

BUILDING YOUR LEADERSHIP TEAM

In business leadership, it is important that you start to see a 'team' in a very different way. Figure 8.1 is a structure I have devised to help you think about who is around you whom you could and should engage with on a regular basis.

Figure 8.1

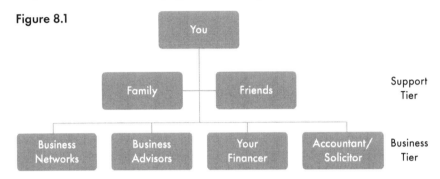

Clearly you are at the helm since it is your business. Importantly I have placed your family and friends as *your support* rather than directly managed by you. They are there to help and guide you, providing an important social network outside of your business. They can 'ground' you when you need it and get you out of bed in the morning when the day looks like too much! I will address these relationships later in the chapter as they may not always be the best people to provide solid business advice. Often, they may tell you what they think you want to hear rather than an objective perspective! That is reserved for the *business tier* that you directly manage — the professional advisors and your peer networks.

The Business Tier

The business tier incorporates the people who you can speak with and test out your ideas and thinking. If you don't use this tier, I would have real concerns as to how you could possibly grow a successful business. We all need a team and this tier is your professional sounding block where you can trust the feedback you are going to get. Trust runs to the core of every business and operates on so many levels of successful business leadership. The key forms of trust in successful business leadership include:

✓ Trust in your leadership, and your staff will exude confidence
✓ Trust in your business, and suppliers, investors and financers will support you

Importantly, you should aim to engage with someone from this tier at least once every two weeks throughout your business life.

TIPS AND IDEAS

Encourage your team to view each other as individuals with lives, ambitions, families and hobbies. Create a culture where people in your business are interested in each other as people and not working robots.

Business Networks

A business network, as illustrated in Figure 8.2, is where you engage with other businesses to share information and possibly even collaborate to become more competitive or innovative in what you do.[15] By being part of a (or several) business network(s) you are able to maximise your knowledge and information through others. It is a great way to learn and you may also get a few new customers along the way.

It is important to remember that business networks can be web-based or work through social media channels. Appreciating that as a business leader your time is precious, it is important that you network effectively and get as much from the process as possible. Figure 8.3 provides specific reasons why business networks are important to each Executive Identity.

Figure 8.2

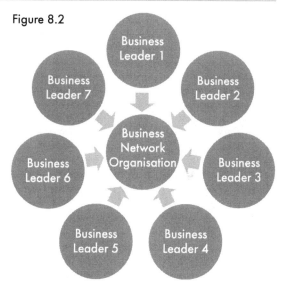

On my travels, I have listened to many business leaders worry about business networking. The main reason is that there is a concern about exposing their business ideas to others in business networks. They are reluctant to attend business meetings and events based on a fear that other business leaders (or indeed the event organisers) may get too much of an insight into their business. The main concern is about alerting any potential competition to their next move. This is particularly true with Blue-Skyers or Academics, where their work can be at the R&D or prototype stage, and there is a concern that ideas can be stolen. It is important to get a few things straight.

Of course, you must ensure that proper intellectual property (IP) and trademarks are put in place as your product development requires. Outside of that, in my experience business leaders are just too involved in their own day-to-day issues to really focus on the finer details of your next move. They have their own products and services to attend to and are also unlikely to have either the knowledge or wherewithal to have any interest in your idea. If you really are that concerned, then just don't share what you don't want people to know. That doesn't stop you from networking and picking up useful tips on how to do business better.

Figure 8.3

Blue-Skyer	You need others to progress your ideas and support your business growth.
Descendant	You need objective opinions outside your own family to keep a wider perspective.
Dabbler	You may think you have all the experience you need but you don't. Ask others for their opinion and draw your own conclusion.
Hobbyist	Make sure to build a wide network, not just other hobbyists.
Progressor	You need to build your own networks over and above those in your last employ.
Academic	Non-academic networks are important.
Lifer	Entrepreneurship and social relationships do not always sit comfortably together, so force yourself to listen to others.
Game Changer	Find business relationships, as those passionate about your cause will always find you.

Case in Point

I have facilitated many business workshops. I have yet to undertake a feedback session at the end of the day where the participants have not remarked on what they have learnt from each other as much as from the information presented to them.

TIPS AND IDEAS

It is important to make the most of your networking opportunities and here are a few Dos and Don'ts:

Do	Don't
Try to engage with other business leaders where you may have a synergy – so do your homework on the network	Don't propel your business card into another's hand
Raise your profile by attending as many events as possible	Make sure not to overexpose the details of your business

Aim for a diverse set of business leaders where you can learn and develop your skills and knowledge	Stand alone – you are there to mix with others so find someone to chat to
Have a genuine interest in others and actively listen	Attend an event without a specific goal
Practise selling yourself through an elevator pitch (i.e. you have the time from the first to the tenth floor to explain to the other person in the lift what it is your business does!)	
Find areas of common interest with others	

Business Advisors

Business Advisors are an interesting bunch. As there really is no regulation on what constitutes a business advisor, they come to a business support role with a variety of knowledge, skills and experience. In theory, a business advisor should be a consultant who provides you with information and knowledge that will support you to operate your businesses better. However, in my experience their quality differs greatly from one advisor to the next. As an Academic you have probably seen more than most in terms of quality. They can range from retired businesspeople to business tutors to public sector employees who have never had any exposure to business, but with marketing and financial advice in bucket loads! Generally, they don't even carry ID.

Yet, most business leaders tend to give them a free run of their premises and the inner workings of their business without too much prompting. Within the first 15 minutes of arriving on a business premises I usually have a full background on the owner, productivity, exports, customers, suppliers and sometimes family. I'm not sure if it is because the entrepreneur has the rare opportunity to discuss their business to someone who is actually listening – possibly!

Please be conscious that as a business leader you are vulnerable to unqualified, unscrupulous advisors and it is in your interests to gather some important background details on anyone you intend to let into the inner workings of your business. If you are coming to business with a limited knowledge of 'business', perhaps like the Progressor, then you are particularly vulnerable. Later in this section I will provide you with an important checklist to support your choice of advisor – please use it, always!

There is another important point I also wish to make here. When we speak with business advisors and those there to support the start-up and growth of business, discussions are usually centred around generic business goals:

✓ Who are your customers?
✓ What are your projected figures?
✓ What skills will you need to develop your business?

In working your way through this book, you will by now have defined your main Executive Identity. Although it is up to you to choose who you might share this with, I strongly advise you share it with your business advisor. If you are paying an advisor to assist you in the growth of your business, letting them know your Executive Identity will provide another important dimension to your mentoring process. It should provide key discussion points around your decision-making and leadership choices. Figure 8.4 provides a key to the specific strategic emphasis that needs to be placed during the mentoring process for each Executive Identity.

Apart from the obvious benefits, I suggest it also ensures you get better value for money in your business advice!

Figure 8.4

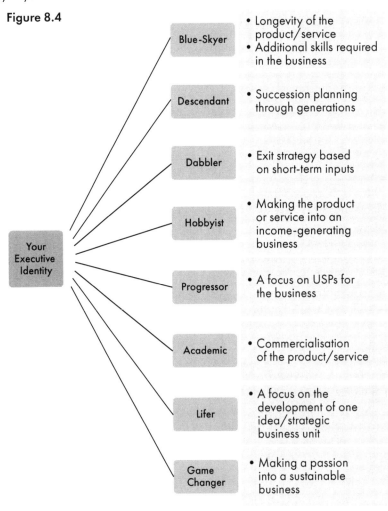

TIPS AND IDEAS

The following is a checklist I strongly suggest you use prior to engaging with any business advisor and before you agree to any on-site meeting at your premises.

Business Advisor Checklist

	Details	Rationale
1.	Who are they? Name, company name, address, email, telephone	Basic contact details
2.	Number of years as a business advisor?	This provides an indication of knowledge. Someone who has worked with businesses for twenty years will have a lot more experience than someone with one year
3.	What professional business qualifications do they have?	When knowledge backs up experience it's usually a good combination
4.	Size of businesses normally advised?	Advising a small business is very different to advising a multinational
5.	What business sectors have they worked with in the past?	To assess experience in your sector
6.	What functional areas of expertise do they have? Marketing, finance, HR, etc.	You can match up your needs with advisors who focus on the needs of your business at that particular point in time. Is it financial, marketing, legal, HR, or information and communications technology (ICT) advice you need just now?
7.	Provide a list of your competitors and check if the advisor has worked with any of them or similar types of businesses	It is important you provide the list as others may not class a business as a competitor without having an insight into your business. It is very important you are aware of any conflicts of interest. Business advisors can have many different business interests and shareholdings, and these are not always disclosed unless you ask
8.	Request the advisor signs a confidentiality agreement	To ensure what's talked about in your meetings stays in your meetings!

The idea of this checklist will be new to many advisors, but if they are uncomfortable or unwilling to engage in the process, then I suggest you find someone else rather quickly!

Your Financer

This is a relationship business leaders often give little attention to – at their peril. Most business leaders look for some level of finance to start their business, from an overdraft for operating costs to a loan for capital investment. Once the initial start-up lending is secured there is little to no further contact with the finance house until more lending is required. There is not even any effort to examine the terms of the lending or to rene-gotiate more favourable terms when the business has proved its survival. Traditional sources are predominately used, including banks, building societies (although I argue that these are for house mortgages!) and small business government loans. I will look later in more detail at equity investment, but for now let's consider these.

When you start out in business you are vulnerable. You are asking a finance house, e.g. a bank, to take a punt on you and to lend you finance based on you – your knowl-edge, experience, passion and (hopefully) a decent business plan. In relative terms your negotiating position is weak and I believe it is even more difficult for Hobbyists as you need to prove your business idea more than others. With little choice (and they know this), most entrepreneurs will sign on the dotted line as the business needs food (i.e. finance) to get going. There really isn't a lot that can be done to change this sce-nario and resistance is futile.

However, all things being equal, hopefully, after not too long and certainly within three years, it is likely this position has changed. Investors and bankers don't usually invest in just premises, products and cash flows; they also look at the abilities of the business leader. If there are still tight reins in your terms after two or three years in business, then you need to examine the way your business operates. The bottlenecks are likely to be your adherence to payment deadlines, the lack of consistency in the quality of your product or the fact that either you or your team are over-promising but under-delivering to your customers. That aside, after you have survived the hardship of start-up you have something new – a business financial history – and this puts you in a much stronger position to negotiate.

The other issue I want to highlight is the ownership of your business. I can hear you saying, 'what do you mean – I own my business'. Well yes, except I want to discuss 'silent shareholding'. That is, if your business owes money to a finance house, then that portion of your business depends on their silent shareholding. Let's say the bank has funded 50 per cent of the tangible assets (buildings and equipment) in your business and these are worth 25 per cent of overall business value, then really the bank (silently) owns 25 per cent of your business. If they call in their lending, then you need to find 25 per cent of the value, in cash – and quickly! Why then is this a relationship you would not want to develop and nurture?

There are of course times when trying to develop this relationship may be outside of your control. Take for example our last global recession. At this time banks and others wanted to distance themselves from their business customers and withdrew many of their executives and replaced them with faceless processes to enable them to call in their loans. However, these unique circumstances aside, I still believe that developing and working these relationships are important. When dealing with finance, Figure 8.5 outlines particular considerations that you may wish to consider for each Executive Identity:

Figure 8.5

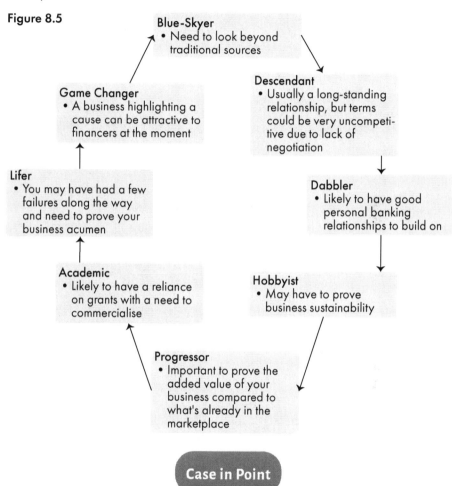

Blue-Skyer
• Need to look beyond traditional sources

Descendant
• Usually a long-standing relationship, but terms could be very uncompetitive due to lack of negotiation

Game Changer
• A business highlighting a cause can be attractive to financers at the moment

Dabbler
• Likely to have good personal banking relationships to build on

Lifer
• You may have had a few failures along the way and need to prove your business acumen

Academic
• Likely to have a reliance on grants with a need to commercialise

Hobbyist
• May have to prove business sustainability

Progressor
• Important to prove the added value of your business compared to what's already in the marketplace

Case in Point

I have worked with many financial houses to secure funding for businesses at their start-up or growth stages. However, I can count on one hand the number of businesses that had any ongoing, long-term, mutually respectful relationships. Those that did reduced the decision-making process on granting further funding by at least half. It makes sense that if the financer knows the business then they need less additional information at the point of commitment.

TIPS AND IDEAS

1. Buying money is like buying anything else your business needs. You need to shop around and barter, and your business is now at the point where you can do this. I'm sure you wouldn't invest €10,000 in equipment without shopping around. So why not for your money?
2. Revisit your relationship with your finances at least once per year and take the opportunity to shop around for better deals, if only to renegotiate better terms for your existing arrangement.
3. Meet with your financial representative once per year. Invite them to visit your company. Show them around and reassure them their investment is secure.

The Investor

So now, as promised, let's take a closer look at the investor – the business angel, venture capitalist or crowd funder. In all the businesses I have worked with, without exception, investors are engaged because finance is required. In this relationship you will give up a share of your business for a financial injection from this source. For some entrepreneurs this may be the only source of finance available to grow the business – common for Hobbyists, Game Changers and Progressors. For others it is a choice and common in their industry, including Blue-Skyers.

I'm a great believer in business leaders considering owning a percentage of something rather than all of nothing! That said, there are important points to make about this relationship. Investors are usually not prepared to lose any of their money; quite the opposite, they will be looking to gain at least five to six times their initial investment within five years. Venture capitalists will probably look for even higher multiples, but are more likely to risk higher levels of investment.

A word of caution with venture capital. We operate in a global environment where the rules of engagement are changing with pace. Before the recession of 2008, most businesses could borrow capital and operating funds with relative ease. Those same businesses are now operating on their own cash flow and their ability to borrow is next to zero. Neither scenario is useful as we needed more checks and balances before the recession and greater access to funding now. Again, we are shaping up to have the same issues, if not more intense, as we emerge from the Covid-19 pandemic. Hence, we have the emergence and significant growth of another player – the venture capitalist.

I saw a recent post on Twitter from one such company looking for new businesses in which they could invest with a warning that they only wanted business leaders to come forward who were prepared to allocate 49 per cent of shareholding in the business to the venture capital company. It's hard to see how that will not become a takeover in a short space of time and any existing business leader will find it hard to be motivated for 51 per cent shareholding. Although this is not always the case, it is worth understanding the nuts and bolts of any financial deal you may undertake.

Unlike traditional finance houses, an investor, by definition, is investing and therefore has an interest in how the business is progressing. So, the investor is also likely to have things to say about what you do and how you do it – but then again that's partly why you need them involved. An investor needs to bring something else to your business, over and above money. With the right finance and investment expertise your business can really thrive.

TIPS AND IDEAS

If you are choosing an investor, then examine the person in detail, not just their money. The following provides a checklist of things you should consider, over and above finance, when choosing an investor.

Choosing an investor checklist: make sure that you satisfied yourself with the answers to these questions for any investor you are considering for your business. Then answer each of these questions honestly on a scale of 1–5 with 5 being the highest score.

1.	What is your opinion of their knowledge and experience in relation to what your business needs?	
2.	What is their attitude to further shareholding at a later stage in the business?	
3.	What is their attitude to other shareholders at a later stage in the business?	
4.	How long are they prepared to lend their money before looking for a return?	
5.	How 'hands on' do they want to be?	
6.	How 'hands on' do you want them to be?	

Accountants and Solicitors

It would be easy to dismiss this group into 'ask around on their reputation and chose one', believing your main interaction with this group will be on a 'need to use' basis. Or as a Dabbler, you may have had a few personal dealings with this group and know someone you have always used. I would challenge that this is much too simplistic an approach for a successful entrepreneur.

This could very well be a relatively ad hoc relationship being used only when required, and yet the enormity of the input can be very far-reaching both personally and in business. The experience of a solicitor in putting the detail into a property purchase contract, for example, can mean business longevity rather than bankruptcy. The ability of an accountant to know what business expenditure is eligible for tax deductions can ensure your business presents the correct tax returns and you remain free of fines. Figure 8.6 provides some key considerations when appointing accountants and solicitors for each Executive Identity.

Figure 8.6

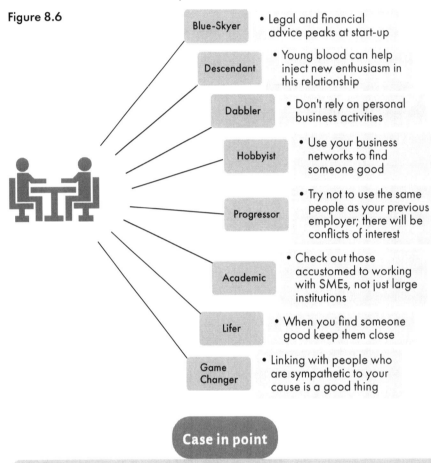

Blue-Skyer
- Legal and financial advice peaks at start-up

Descendant
- Young blood can help inject new enthusiasm in this relationship

Dabbler
- Don't rely on personal business activities

Hobbyist
- Use your business networks to find someone good

Progressor
- Try not to use the same people as your previous employer; there will be conflicts of interest

Academic
- Check out those accustomed to working with SMEs, not just large institutions

Lifer
- When you find someone good keep them close

Game Changer
- Linking with people who are sympathetic to your cause is a good thing

Case in point

I once worked with an engineering company that was operating from a leased premises with a rolling ten-year contract. The rental on the lease was very cheap as the company had only leased the shell of the building, but after ten months of renovations and significant capital expenditure the business had a very modern production and administration facility. The business owner was only fourteen months into his contract when the landlord went bankrupt and the building was seized by the bank. Fortunately for the business owner, his solicitor had a clause in the lease contract that stated that he could have first refusal to buy the building if it ever went on sale. That clause saved his bacon and allowed him to acquire the building and continue to trade for many years to come rather than being turned out by a new landlord, with little or no compensation for the massive outlay on the internal workings of the building.

TIPS AND IDEAS

1. It is important to appreciate that a solicitor good at devising wills may not be the best person to negotiate your ten-year property lease on the high street or the development of your employment contracts. It is not a one-size-fits-all scenario and it is important to choose a business solicitor and accountant with the appropriate business experience.
2. There is also a huge variation in pricing structure with different firms and even individuals within firms who charge different hourly rates – so make sure you shop around.

The Support Tier

Family

My definition of family is whatever that means to you – co-parent, single parent, sibling looking after other siblings with no parents – or any other combination you can think of. The definition is irrelevant. What is relevant is the fact that you are leading a business while also linking with a family in the process. So, what are the common reasons why your relationships with family change when you go into business leadership?

Whether you asked for it or not, there will be pivotal points in these relationships when you need to manage many levels of personal life, family life and business life. Like the seesaw in Figure 8.7, a pivot can often feel isolating, with you needing to balance many demands from business and family.

Figure 8.7

Importantly, there are times when the seesaw may be out of balance: there are times in life when you may need to pay more attention to one or the other depending on what curve balls are thrown your way. The key is that these remain short-term and temporary, as anything else could result in irreversible relationship damage. Being aware that some situations are 'normal' and making sure they remain temporary is the key to leading a successful business with your family relationships intact.

As a business leader, you need to notice that you are generally wrapped up in your company. For example, the business at start-up is like a newborn and needs a lot of attention. It can be all-consuming and may mean you have less time for the everyday demands of family life. By the time you get home you have little energy left to deal with the homework or friendship issues of your thirteen-year-old. The temptation is to work long days and the pressure of needing to make sales and ensure a family lifestyle can make this need feel more intense.

Case in Point

When you invest some of your profits back into new product development rather than into a savings account to help cover the cost of sending your child to university, or a family holiday to Disney World, you are making a choice – for everyone. What seems like a choice you should make alone, as it's your business, is suddenly not just your choice. From my experience business leaders are fairly selfish and take little or no cognisance of their nearest and dearest other than the fleeting thought that they will benefit from all the (definite) successes ahead! Then they wonder why their family is not always there for them in the long run.

TIPS AND IDEAS

1. You must put structure into your day as early in the process as possible and certainly within the first six weeks. The hours you work in any day will depend on the type of business you operate and the markets you are targeting. Regardless, you need a routine and your family need to know what part of the day you are available and paying attention to only them.
2. As the business develops and grows, then there are other considerations. The balance of your priorities, particularly time and finance, are a challenge.
3. When leading your business becomes the norm for everyone connected to you, it becomes difficult to separate your business decisions from your family. The actions and behaviour of you, the leader, become infused with the development of the business and the family. After all, you, and usually you alone, are making the decisions and taking the rest of your family along for the ride.
4. It Is very easy to justify your business decisions as the requirement of your *business*. Although this is true you need to be mindful that with limited resources, i.e. time and finance, your decisions are also having a direct impact on your nearest and dearest. You should involve your family in your pivotal decisions and at least listen to their point of view before that final curtain call.

A Spotlight on the Descendant

I come from the school of thinking that the lack of long-term success of generational businesses is down to the breakdown of family relationships both inside and outside the business. For you, the Descendant, relationships are complex. You are being asked to invert your natural instincts. By that I mean the majority of the population go to their working day which is devoid of family members and then come home to relax with family. You are asking yourself to do the opposite. In addition to the normal 'business team', your family are not just assistants to your business life, as a Descendant at least some of these assistants will also be in business with you. You may even be working with the previous generation, siblings and even maybe the next generation or a few cousins – all in your everyday business life! Maintaining those relationships inside and outside the business is a unique challenge for you.

Like everyone else in business you need to ensure that you maintain the external relationships I refer to in this chapter. However, you have additional needs, and regardless of where you are in the generational transition of the business, there are some tips and ideas you can put in place to smooth the way.

1. Treat family members the same as any other director or employee in the company.
2. Ensure each family member has their formal titles, roles and responsibilities just like anyone else, and make sure these are communicated across the business – to both family and non-family members.
3. Although difficult, it is important to place family emotions aside and deal with each family member in an objective and professional way. Just because you knew the person when they wore nappies doesn't mean that you treat them any differently.
4. Leave family issues at home and deal with business issues in business, and ensure others do likewise.
5. Make sure not to create a 'them and us' culture. 'Them' being non-family employees and 'us' being family members. It will create a toxic environment in the long run.
6. Restrict the number of family members in the business, particularly at senior management/director level, and continue to recruit employees and professionals to support growth.
7. Gather up a loyal set of friends so you can socialise outside the family and get a different perspective on life.

Friendships

I must say, I tend to agree with the saying 'there are no friends in business'. This doesn't mean you can't have friends and be in business. These are two very different things. The former refers to involving your friends in your business, the latter refers to having and keeping your friends separate to your business – much the same as anyone keeps their work separate to their friendships.

In my experience, having friends involved in your business is OK provided you are willing to sacrifice the friendship. It's not always a negative experience, but it is always a challenging one. If you must muddy the water, then I want to examine two common scenarios.

When a friend becomes an employee, they are an employee and the relationship has changed for good. It's like watching a powerful film: once you have watched it you cannot go back, it is forever in your psyche. Like working with family, you now need to manage the friendship (and the friendships of their connected network) both inside and outside your business. This is not impossible, and I can think of examples where friends become a loyal set of eyes and ears in your business. In the music industry, some may argue it's crucial to have a group of close loyal employees who are friends to ensure you remain grounded and focused. For example, Chris Martin, the lead singer in Coldplay, has successfully surrounded himself with friends in key positions on his team and wouldn't have it any other way. Yet it's a small team with few other employees and mainly external advisors.

The other most common example of friends in business is as a business partner. There are many friendships that end up in business. As this is a more 'equal' relationship, in some ways it can be easier than the employer–employee relationship. The advantages are that you know the person before you go into business together and you can see where you compliment (and clash) with each other. The disadvantage is you may be too close and have very high and unrealistic expectations of each other. The most common argument I have witnessed is which partner has put more into the business (finance, effort, time) and therefore should get more out.

Case in Point

I was working with a hairdressing business a few years back. There were two partners in the business and they had been friends since nursery school. With quite different personalities they were able to manage their team and customers very effectively; one paying great attention to detail and the other being a real 'people person'. When I worked with them both, they had been in business for 25 years. The business now employed one of the children of one of the partners and this was changing the dynamic and their friendship for the worse. In addition, the son and the parent wanted the son to take over the business and this was causing significant tension with the other business partner, who was beginning to feel pushed out. As with most situations in life, I encouraged both partners to step back and look at the business in an objective way. After a few 'away days' examining what they both wanted and where the business was heading, the vision became quite clear. Both partners wanted to retire! So, we had the business independently and objectively valued, the son took out a loan and bought both his parent and her friend out. The icing on the cake was that the two business partners maintained their long-term friendship.

TIPS AND IDEAS

1. If you must have friends involved in your business, then you must be prepared to work harder through the challenges you meet if you wish to maintain the friendship.
2. If you are taking friends on as employees be open and honest with them before you recruit them. Make sure you both understand the lines between work and friendship, and discuss each other's expectations.
3. Ensure friends are introduced into your business like any other employee and avoid favouritism at all costs. See the Summary Exercise below.
4. Keep being social.

SUMMARY EXERCISE

It is important that you identify who is currently involved, who you need to be involved and how you are going to bridge this gap.

Please fill out the following chart in two separate ways.

Complete the chart in Figure 8.8, naming the key people who currently exist in your relationships and who are important for you and your business.

Figure 8.8

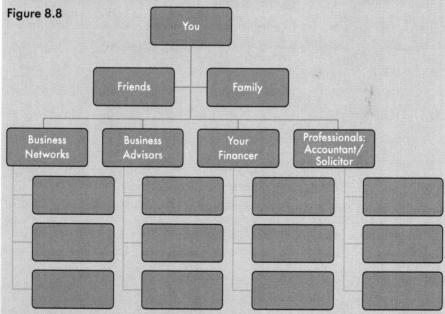

Complete the chart in Figure 8.9 naming the key people who you need for you and your business.

Complete the action plan below Figure 8.9 to identify how you are going to start to build these relationships in the next twelve months.

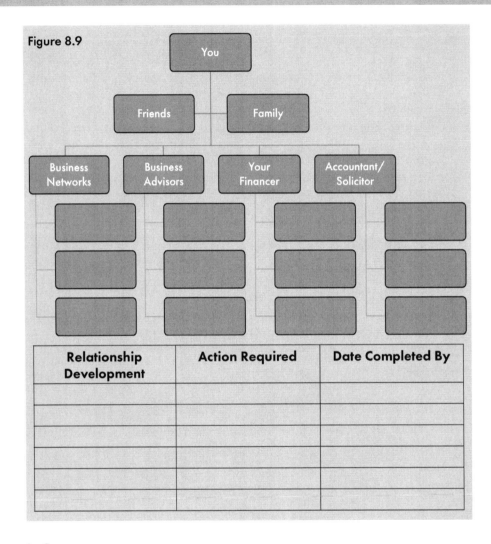

Figure 8.9

Relationship Development	Action Required	Date Completed By

IN SUMMARY

As we all know, relationships can be rewarding and complicated at the same time. They can also change with time and with the individuals involved. Relationships that you have as a business leader are no exception and some people are naturally more sociable than others in life and so also in business.

However, there is plenty of evidence to show that business leaders tend to believe they are more isolated than their non-business peers or indeed their employees. For this reason, you need to work hard to build and maintain your professional relationships as there is no doubt that every business leader needs them. Your Executive Identity will also have an impact on how you form and maintain your relationships and it should be something you are aware of and work with.

9

JUST YOU

'The Pessimist complains about the wind. The Optimist expects it to change. The Leader adjusts the sails.'

John Maxwell, author

KEY CHAPTER POINTS

- ✓ You are the key to business success.
- ✓ Your personal health is the key to your leadership success.
- ✓ Changing small ways of working can have large impacts on your wellbeing.
- ✓ Taking care of yourself.

We started this book by examining the importance of you at the helm of your business – starting, growing, sustaining and reinventing your business and your leadership. You are the core of it all and the most important individual in your business world. We have discovered along the way there are also many others who rely on you for their success – your staff, suppliers, customers, investors and not least your family. Looking after yourself is not selfish – in fact quite the opposite. It makes total business sense that you should look after the biggest asset your business has and investing in your wellbeing is investing in the longevity and success of your business.

It is often stated that 'your health is your wealth' and indeed so it is. Working alongside so many business leaders has afforded me the opportunity to see so many combinations of working patterns from the balanced to the completely unsustainable regime. I have witnessed business leaders with real positive attitudes based on good health and an understanding of where business fits in their lives, and also those who are completely swamped and in poor health just fighting to keep it all together. The former are thriving in business while the latter are working their way out – and quickly. There are a number of factors that can impact on how you look after yourself and not least your personal circumstances, wealth, age and access to health care. It is never too late to start to invest in yourself. Each Executive Identity will also be particularly prone to certain stresses and strains, and these will be explored here.

THE BLUE-SKYER

A workaholic by nature, you can operate in a fast and frenzied business day, working with highs and lows and sometimes taking one step forward to take two steps back. Yours is not a calm world either internally or physically in your working environment. Constantly striving towards the next Dyson or Facebook can be draining and demanding, and you can expect a lot from yourself both physically and mentally. As in Figure 9.1, your predictable working day split into work time and 'me time' can look something like this.

It doesn't matter that up to now you may have skipped breakfast, drank copious amounts of coffee all day and stayed at work late every evening. You can take control of your life and make time for the things that matter to you, but nobody else is going to do that for you. It has to start with you. What matters is that this stops as of now.

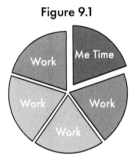

Figure 9.1

Going back to my Physics lessons in school, I remember running a stress test on a sample of metal. What we did was bend the metal until such point as it broke and then we recorded the pressure it took to reach that breaking point. We are far from being a piece of metal, but I think the sentiment is the same. There is such a thing as 'good stress', often referred to as 'eustress'. This is a type of mild stress that we can all experience on a regular basis and instead of being debilitating it is motivating and can propel your thinking forward. As a Blue-Skyer you will be familiar with this description. The crucial difference between this and 'bad stress' is that it is short-term and temporary, such as preparing and delivering a speech to a large audience. Eustress is actually necessary to motivate us in certain circumstances and help us to find solutions to a temporary problem.

'Bad stress' or distress is when you experience ongoing prolonged exposure to difficult situations and when you have adverse pressure placed on you. This can lead to a state of physical, mental and emotional exhaustion, meaning you are unable to keep up with your everyday commitments and operate your business effectively. You are the Executive Identity that can be particularly affected by bad stress, leaving you much more susceptible to infections, coughs and much more serious illnesses. Like the piece of metal in my experiment, if the stress continues uncontrolled, then eventually you could break, suffering from burnout.

TIPS AND IDEAS

There are a number of warning signs you should be aware of before becoming over-stressed. The key is for you to be aware of the warning signs and to act to prevent any further deterioration. By addressing these warning signs and alleviating the pressure you could prevent a tsunami in your personal and business life:

✓ Being irritable or impatient
✓ Being overly anxious – perhaps waking up at night with anxious thoughts
✓ Racing thoughts and not being able to switch off
✓ Being unable to enjoy yourself and uninterested in life
✓ Having a sense of dread
✓ Feeling neglected or lonely
✓ Feeling over-burdened with risk

EXERCISE

List the issues that are causing you stress and the actions you could take to minimise them and thus reduce stress.

Issue	Action	Completed By

THE DESCENDANT

As the Descendant you have come into business leadership where there is already an established culture and norms. It can be stressful to be the family member coming into the business and trying to make your mark. It can be easy for you to believe that you need to fill your day with tasks and activities that have always been done – the norms. A bit like the theory set out by Parkinson's Law (first noted by Cyril Parkinson in 1955),[16] which states that the more time we choose to dedicate to a particular task, the longer it will take to complete. The theory goes that even if we could complete the task in a shorter time, we will make the task fit the time we have allocated. So, your tasks can expand to fill the time available and you could end up doing a lot of things right but not necessarily the right things for your business. It is imperative that you make sure to focus on the 20 per cent and maximise your efforts and the efforts of others on your team.

Case in Point

Around ten years ago I walked into a family-run farm diversification food manufacturing business with twenty employees. The business leader was in his mid-60s and was clearly stressed and told me as much. He was working with his doctor to try to deal with anxiety attacks he would have in the middle of the night, when his thoughts would turn to the things he hadn't done during the day. I asked him to work through this diary exercise and this revealed a very interesting pattern. This business leader was spending around one day per week working on invoicing and receipts, physically putting them onto a spreadsheet to create a financial record.

When we discussed that this was not the most effective or efficient use of his time, he was quick to point out that financial knowledge in any business is vital. That he had always done this and it had served him well. I absolutely agreed with him but pointed out that his job was to receive the information and make decisions based on the information – not inputting the data into a spreadsheet. I then quickly went on to work out the cost implications. He was taking €40,000/year of salary from the business – so his daily salary was €40,000/6x52 (based on a six-day working week) = €128/day. So, his admin role was costing the business €6,656/year (€128 x 52) – enough I would have thought to employ a part-time administrator and allow the business leader to get some much-needed non-work time.

EXERCISE

Step 1 – In order to understand if you are having an issue with your work and life it is useful to start by keeping a diary. Keep a diary for a week – an average typical week rather than any specific week. Break your day into three-hour slots and record what you are generally doing during those three hours. Foremost, I suggest you use the following categories:

✓ Working slots broken down into:
  ° Admin
  ° The managing function (planning, coordinating, directing)
  ° The commercial function (production, marketing, finance)
  ° The entrepreneurial function (risk-taking, decision-making, innovation)
✓ Life slots broken down into:
  ° Chores (cooking, school run, cleaning)
  ° Me time (exercise, reading, listening to music, etc.)
  ° Fun (activities with kids, socialising, friends, etc.)
  ° Sleep

By looking back over this diary, you will most likely be very surprised with some patterns, including:

✓ Wasting too much time at work on making yourself busy with tasks that others can do
✓ Not enough me time or fun in your personal life
✓ Not enough sleep

Step 2 – Think about how you would like your life to look. What would be your perfect time at work and non-work? Then make a list of the changes you need to make to create this position.

Step 3 – Implement the changes.

THE HOBBYIST

One of your challenges is to try to bring about more balance, given the stage your business is at and the fact that you can get 'stuck' in your comfort zone at business start. Also, because you tend to work from home more often than any of the other Executive Identities, the lines between work and home can become blurred. It can be difficult to switch off and get away from the office because it's next door to the kitchen! You are the most likely of all the Executive Identities to have the perception that you always need to be busy doing something and you also like to hang onto the things you like doing, rather than the things that need to be done. Once you have a picture of how your life separates out, you are better informed to make the changes you need to protect yourself from long-term damage and ultimately improve the balance in your life.

EXERCISE

This exercise uses the Eisenhower Matrix[17] – a model for time management that compares the urgency and importance of tasks to assist you to set priorities.

	URGENT	**NOT URGENT**
IMPORTANT	DO – Important and Urgent	SCHEDULE – Important but not Urgent
NOT IMPORTANT	DELEGATE – Important but not Urgent	ELIMINATE – Not Important and Not Urgent

Complete this box on a Sunday evening or Monday morning and stick to it for your working week.

THE DABBLER

As the Dabbler you can be an investor in a business or equally leading a business that is not within your industry knowledge or expertise. This can mean that you have the sense that many of the business leadership issues you are dealing with are not totally within your control on a fairly continuous basis. This can range from losing a main supplier to an underperforming key employee and anything in between. Allowing yourself to become frustrated with issues over which you believe you have limited control can cause your frustration to rise and your confidence to subside. There are many aspects in business that can lead us to become disillusioned and many are often beyond our control. For example, the Covid-19 pandemic was virtually impossible to plan for. Unfortunately, as the Dabbler, the number of issues can be endless and sometimes totally external and definitely beyond your control. Thankfully you can control your approach and develop ways to deal with these situations when they arise. Your positive thinking needs to be able to prevail even in times of greater uncertainty.

Case in Point

I have worked with many Dabblers. However, one in particular stands out for her persistence and success. Having taken over a retail business this entrepreneur wanted to enjoy a good life. From her 20s she enjoyed her coffee mornings, golfing and general 'me time'. There is no doubt the business could have generated significantly greater returns over her reign with just a little more attention. Frustratingly for those who wanted to lend her money to expand, that just wasn't what the owner was looking for. This changed overnight when the recession hit in 2008. With retail taking one of the hardest hits, this entrepreneur, now in her 40s, moved at lightning speed. I've never seen someone move so fast! The golf clubs went into storage and the helicopter landed. The business was restructured and consolidated within weeks. Very specific targets were set for income, staffing, customers and product. A thriving retail business exists today with a huge destination customer and is already moving on to the next generation. The moral of the story – no-one should underestimate a Dabbler as quite often they are still surviving when others have failed!

EXERCISE

This exercise has two steps:

1. Fill in the boxes in Figure 9.2 with situations that are impacting on your business leadership where you have limited or no control. I want you to consider issues such as expertise, your relationship with suppliers, bank lending and so on.

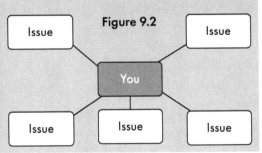

Figure 9.2

2. List each impact here and identify the actions you need to take to reduce its impact on your business leadership. Then identify the date for completion.

Issue	Actions to Reduce Impact	Completed By

THE LIFER

> 'Success is failure turned inside out – the silver tint of the clouds of doubt, and you never can tell how close you are, it may be near when it seems so far; so stick to the fight when you're hardest hit – it's when things seem worst that you must not quit. For of all sad words of tongue or pen, the saddest are these: "It might have been!"'
> John Greenleaf Whittier, poet (1807–1892)

As the Lifer, we have mentioned many times your capacity to look diversity in the eye and move forward with an inherent tenacity for success. Yet, I have worked with a number of Lifers and one of the common drivers in their leadership is a fear of failure. At what point is something not working for you?

Is success just around the corner if only you had a little more finance, patience or time? When is it time to call it a day?

If you have had previous business 'failures' then you need to be prepared to defend the circumstances and reasons for that failure. There are many people in business who appreciate that when a Lifer hits adversity and shows their tenacity to work through their adversity that is a positive thing. I suggest that failure is really when a business does not meet its objectives and targets, and you should be bound to setting specific strategic targets for the business and stick to these. Developing a detailed and realistic business plan is a good start. Quick and decisive action is the key when targets are not being met. Swift addressing of the issues or a redirection may not only save the business but propel it forward.

TIPS AND IDEAS

1. Having a detailed business plan with specific objectives and targets will reduce the fear of failure as you will get plenty of warning signs that things are not moving along according to plan.
2. When you are writing your targets reflect on your fears and write targets around this. For example, if your fear is bankruptcy then your business target needs to have all your operational debt paid within 45 days and your loan repayments on time. Then if you see this moving in the wrong direction you know to sit up and pay a lot of attention. It may be time to look at reinvention on the business life cycle.
3. The key to turning failure into success in business leadership is informed, quick and decisive actions to deal with the problems.

THE PROGRESSOR

As the Progressor you can often get caught up with everyone's issues both inside and outside of work. There is a high probability that you took staff with you into your business from your previous employment and you tend to have a number of 'friends' on your team. We have discussed the problems this can create in Chapter 8, in that it can make it difficult to separate friendship and management. Saying 'No' to your team can be a problem for you. This can lead to a stressful environment if not brought into check, as you can be guilty of trying to please everyone while pleasing no one, including yourself. It is important that you lead in an assertive way that gains the respect of your team, customers and key stakeholders. Assertiveness in leadership is a highly valued trait as it encourages direct, calm communication that maintains long-term, good relationships. When you are assertive, you respect yourself and others and so it is a good leadership quality that you need to practice, get comfortable with and use. It has the capacity to make your business leadership and your business a lot stronger.

TIPS AND IDEAS

1. Practice speaking openly, starting your sentences with, 'I think,' 'I feel,' 'I notice'. Within a very short time this will come to you as second nature.
2. Start to actively listen to your team. This means just that – listen. Don't be thinking about what you are going to say when they are finished speaking – just listen.
3. Learn to say 'No'.

THE ACADEMIC

As the Academic, you can get very consumed by the development of your research. Your view can be tunnelled, just looking at problems and trying to find solutions. Your existence in business can be fairly insular, until you get to at least the growth stage. Like the Hobbyist, you may be working at home on your own, but more likely you are working in an educational setting. Engaging with others either on a business or personal level is important for your overall health. This will enable you to lift your head and get some much-needed change of scenery. I also suggest that you engage in some positive thinking space, i.e. taking time out to think positively, both strategically and operationally, in your working day. This can be very productive, involving getting away from your usual workspace – maybe taking a walk or lying in the bath and just thinking about the problem and possible solutions, taking a little breathing space when you need it. This is a really effective technique that is completely underused in our leadership bag of tricks. Business leaders sometimes view this as wasting time and it's anything but!

Case in Point

I once worked with a colleague who was working up a strategic plan for a central government department. They had stumbled across a difficult problem in their meeting and had already spent the morning trying to come up with a solution. My colleague asked for the meeting to be adjourned as she wanted to take a walk in the local park. When asked was she feeling ok my colleague said 'perfectly, I am just going to have some strategic thinking time and will hopefully come up with some options to solve our problem' – and she did take the walk and she did come up with an ingenious solution.

TIPS AND IDEAS

1. It's a good idea to have time in your day when you are technology free and switch off your mobile phone. These devices can make you feel like you are 'always on', which increases your anxiety levels.
2. Think about taking longer periods off after a busy time, so that you benefit from your accomplishments and enjoy relaxing.
3. Try not to stay too long in one place and one position. If you have been sitting at your desk for three hours, get up and walk around. Apart from the benefits of this movement you will be surprised how you can get a different perspective even on the smallest of problems.

THE GAME CHANGER

As the Game Changer your default position is to 'be busy'. We discussed in Chapter 3 how you can get stuck in the growth stage of the business as there is a lot happening at that time. This can lead you to believe that the business is succeeding and could even be mistaken for the maturity stage, but as I highlighted in Chapter 6 its 20 per cent of your effort that will give 80 per cent of the results, and you just need to learn to prioritise your tasks. Without doing so, there is a high possibility that you will get very stressed, less productive overall in your business leadership, and eventually succumb to poor health. Time management allows you to take control of the tasks and activities that you work on every day. If you want to be truly productive and have more time for self, then maybe you need to try to master prioritising your tasks and work on the most productive tasks. By doing so, you are more able to handle another difficult aspect of business leadership – stress.

EXERCISE

To start to think about your balance, consider your response to the following statements:

Statement	Ranking 1–10 (1 = almost never, 10 = almost always)
I forget about work when I'm not working	
I have time every day to spend just on me	
I have interests outside of work	
I generally take a lunch break every day	
I have time for friends at least once per week	
My family are never upset with me about the time I spend at work	

If you answered 5 or less for some or all of these statements, you are likely to benefit from greater balance between work and life.

TIPS AND IDEAS

Here are some ways to try to get a better work– life balance in your life:

✓ Stop checking emails at the weekend and let everyone know.
✓ Have time in your day when you switch off your phone, tablet and computer. If family and friends need to get in contact with you, then buy a separate personal phone.
✓ Have a day in your week that is free of chores.
✓ If nothing else get a 20-minute walk in the fresh air every day.

REMEMBER TO TAKE A HOLIDAY

I want to use holidays as the prime example. I'm really not too sure what it is about us business leaders in the West and our belief that the longer the hours and more days we work, then the more successful we will be. There is almost this idea that taking time for yourself or having a holiday in some way undermines your commitment to your business and its success. In most Western countries, full-time employees are usually entitled to at least five to six weeks' holiday per year on full pay, give or take a few days. This ensures that most people who work get enough time to themselves and keep a balance between work and life.

Generally, when I present these figures to the business leaders I work with, I'm usually met with a blank expression or a chuckle to indicate 'wouldn't that be nice'. I'm not too sure what we expect of ourselves. If I tried to run a machine in the factory non-stop for twelve months, without any downtime, at best its life span would be severely reduced and at worst it would pack up, and who could blame it? If you are expecting that you can keep going and going without a break, then you have unrealistic expectations of yourself and those close to you. If you have a partner and children, it would not be unreasonable that they might feel second-rate to your business if you cannot take a family holiday. When my children were growing up the one thing that was never compromised was the family holiday. I still believe to this day that their learning and exposure to different surroundings, and on many occasions different cultures, made them the rounded young people they are today.

The thing is, there will never be a right time to leave a business. As you well know there are always things that need dealt with, whether at an operational or strategic level. So, the best approach to a holiday is to book it, take it and enjoy it. You can deal with everything else when you get back. Holidays are essential for you to recharge your batteries, refocus your life and get a perspective on your business. They also ensure you maintain good mental health.

SUMMARY EXERCISE

The exercise in Figure 9.3 is designed to assist you to think of how you spend your working day and how you should be spending your working day.

1. On the first clock face, break up your working day as to how much time you currently spend on these tasks:

   - ✓ Planning
   - ✓ Coordinating
   - ✓ Directing
   - ✓ Production
   - ✓ Marketing
   - ✓ Finance
   - ✓ Risk-taking
   - ✓ Decision-making
   - ✓ Innovation

2. On the second clock face show how you need to break up your working day to lead a successful business.

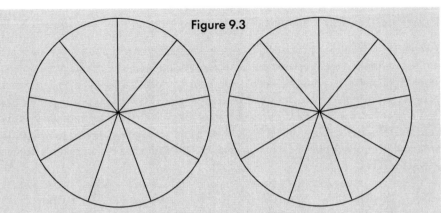

Figure 9.3

3. Complete the following action plan to work on the changes to maximise your time.

Issue for Change	Change to be Made	Completed By

IN SUMMARY

In the twenty-first century we are probably more aware of the need for a positive work–life balance than ever before. There are endless references to it in our daily life and there are a few key aspects that are relevant to highlight for you in your business leadership. As a business leader, the common denominator is often your ability to strike a positive approach. Positive thinking is to be encouraged for all of us from an early age. Encouragement in our qualities from our families, our schools and our communities are where the foundations of a positive attitude need to begin for each of us.

I am a true advocate of this thinking, with a warning. Each and every one of us is unique and as such the power of positive thinking is an individual journey and so our ability to think positively can be affected by so many different variables, from past experiences to the current situation in which we find ourselves. There is a world of difference between encouraging positive thinking and setting unrealistic expectations. The former focuses on the abilities of the child and how they can maximise their abilities, the latter sets the child up for a fall only to believe they are incapable. Realising the personal nature of your Executive Identity will hopefully enable you to get the most from yourself while also living a full and varied life.

10

YOUR EXIT STRATEGY

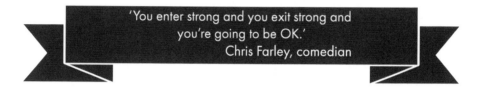

'You enter strong and you exit strong and
you're going to be OK.'
Chris Farley, comedian

KEY CHAPTER POINTS

✓ The key to successful business leadership is knowing your exit strategy from the beginning.
✓ Businesses need to be led in different ways depending on their exit strategy.
✓ Different Executive Identities in the Executive Identity Model® suit different exit strategies.
✓ Understand the warning signs of a business that is declining.

When you start out in your business, usually the last thing on your mind is how you are eventually going to get out of that business. You are so focused on getting it started and working hard to grow it into a success, that the idea of how, or what, you might get out of it at the end is not a priority. You are not alone, as a high percentage of business leaders think in exactly the same way. This can be a real mistake in your business leadership and I want to suggest to you that this should be part of your thinking from the beginning – even at the pre-start-up stage. Ideally the best time to consider your exit strategy is when you are at the ideas generation stage of your business. If that has not been the case, then it's important that you start thinking about it now – without any further delay.

Why? You are putting in a lot of hours, days, weeks and years into building your business and, if for nothing else, you need to know why this is the case. To maintain your own motivation and that of those around you, you need to know your endgame. It's a little like when adults ask a teenager, 'what is it you want to do when you leave school?' The question usually raises one of three answers:

1. No idea.
2. Not sure but I'm thinking of X.
3. I'm going to be a Y.

Now, as much as I'm an advocate for letting children find their feet without too much pressure and providing them with time to move from (1) and (2) to (3), I'm afraid business doesn't tend to afford us that luxury. Unfortunately (1) and (2) are not an option for any business leader and if you're not too sure about what 'you're going to be', then why are you in business? Maybe you should wait until you do. Dithering in business is costly. Not just financially costly, but draining of your valuable time and expertise. As business leaders we don't have a bottomless pit of finance, patience or time, and that is probably a good thing.

There is a popular assumption that all businesses are going to be run as if they will be sold somewhere down the line. It is true that this is probably one of the most popular options for business leaders, but it is certainly not the only one. There are a number of options open to you for consideration, including:

✓ Building the business to sell
✓ Building the business for generations to come
✓ Building the business for a management buy-out
✓ Enabling the business to create your lifestyle to ultimately shut it down and move on

The growth strategy you need to have for your business is very different depending on which of these exit strategies you are working towards, and is more suited to some Executive Identities more than others.

BUILDING THE BUSINESS TO SELL

This is probably the most popular exit strategy for business leaders. The sale is normally to an external buyer, although sometimes you can sell your shares to another shareholder. As set out in Figure 10.1, out of the eight Executive Identities in the Executive Identity Model®, five are particularly suited to this exit strategy.

The following table outlines the rationale for these choices.

Figure 10.1

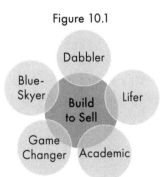

Executive Identity	Rationale
Blue-Skyer	Your business is all about selling. As soon as you get a product or service with traction in the marketplace you tend to be open for business.
Descendant	You are generally handing on to the next generation. It is difficult for any external body to buy into a family business and they are generally only interested if the family members are prepared to sell all their shares.
Hobbyist	The business very much revolves around you and your craft, and without you it would struggle to be a business. It is unlikely that anyone would want to buy into this unless they have the same interest and passion for your craft as you display.
Dabbler	You are normally keen to get your return on your investment within a relatively short period of time (within five years) and so selling is the obvious exit strategy for your business.
Lifer	Your idea of success is selling your business at a significant profit so that you can move onto the next venture.
Progressor	The business is really there to create a lifestyle for you rather than something that is worth very much. You have probably not reinvested too much back into the business to keep the environment up-to-date with the competition. There really is very little for someone to buy.
Academic	As the developer of a product from research, your aim has most likely always been to either sell the business or at least sell the product under some type of arrangement such as licencing.
Game Changer	With the right product and a recognised brand, your business can be attractive to a buyer – much like when L'Oréal bought over The Body Shop. It does tend to be a long-term vision rather than a quick return.

Selling a business for a windfall of cash that can be used for retirement, reinvestment or a different venture is the dream of many business leaders. If this is your strategy, then you need to continuously build your business through the eyes of an external buyer. Here are a few of the main areas a buyer will examine when purchasing your business:

✓ The level of sales and their consistent growth over the past number of years
✓ Consistent net profits
✓ A loyal customer base that will come back after the sale
✓ Brand loyalty (if applicable)

✓ Contracts secured (if applicable)
✓ The popularity of your website
✓ A consistent, tested approach to your production processes
✓ Low staff turnover
✓ Long-standing supplier relationships
✓ Quality of systems and procedures for internal operations and customers

The timing of your sale is everything. You really want to reach a balance in the above points before you consider selling the business to get maximum returns. This makes perfect sense. This doesn't happen by chance but rather it's a planned process that you need to lead and drive. You should also be prepared to work in the business during a 'handover' period – often 12 to 24 months – to assist the new owners to familiarise themselves with all the aspects of the business. This means you may want to consider selling two years earlier than originally planned so you can move on with your life at your set time.

To prepare for this strategy early in the business, I suggest putting in place standard operating procedures for everything from customers' terms of sale to how to clean down the fridge. By working your way through a detailed 'operating manual' for the business you are depersonalising it and the business becomes its own entity, external to your personality. If you standardise what you are doing and how you do it, then anyone can buy and run the business the way you have successfully led it to that point. Whoever buys the business can pick it up where you left off. It is advisable to start this very early in the establishment of the business; of course you can adapt and modify as you go, but if you leave this to before you intend to sell the business it will be very complicated, time-consuming and may even put you off selling the business.

Case in Point

I worked with a retail business many years ago that was operating out of two outlets at the time. The business operated as a partnership and the owners were aware they wanted to grow the business for an ultimate sale through multiply-ing the number of retail outlets and developing a brand. After some discussion, I suggested that they start by creating an operating manual based on the two outlets they owned and the manual should cover every working aspect of the business. This would help them to focus on the operations and support the overall vision to build up and sell on. The manual could be developed as the business grew. The last time I looked the company had opened new outlets and was ready for a buyer to come along with the right offer.

Equally, for those of you who held on to any buy-to-let property during the recession in 2008, you will know only too well that it doesn't always pay to hold on too long waiting for the 'perfect' solution. When to sell a business is not an exact science and it will be affected by many circumstances, including your personal ambitions as a business leader, as well as the market for buyers in your industry.

'If a window of opportunity appears don't pull down the shade.'
Tom Peters, business writer

TIPS AND IDEAS

It is always difficult to put a value on a business – but a rough rule of thumb is to take your average net profit over the past 12 months and then multiply it by a factor of 20–40. This factor will depend on the points I have made and the consistency of your net profit. The longer the history, the higher a factor you could use.

BUILDING THE BUSINESS FOR GENERATIONS TO COME

By building a generational business you are really setting up a business to be here for the long term. The obvious Executive Identity to suit this strategy is the Descendant. However, as set out in Figure 10.2 this can also be an exit strategy for the Lifer (who is most likely to hand over the business and move onto the next project) and the Hobbyist (who passes their craft to the next generation, for example sauce-making moves from mother to daughter).

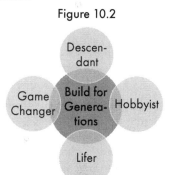

Figure 10.2

Executive Identity	Rationale
Blue-Skyer	Your business strategy tends to be much more short-term. Build it up and sell on.
Descendant	You have taken over a business that has been built to hand on to the next generation.
Hobbyist	It is not unusual for your type of business to be handed on to the next generation. For centuries, crafts have been handed from one generation to the next; it really depends on whether the next generation have an interest in and a flair for the craft.
Dabbler	You tend to be most focused on your own needs and getting a return for your efforts. Another generation does not tend to be a consideration for you.

Lifer	Sometimes you could be interested in handing on to a descendant if the business had enough longevity. However, this does not tend to be your natural go-to exit strategy at the outset.
Progressor	As a lifestyle business leader, you are most likely to just get your income and someday close the door not to return.
Academic	Your business really doesn't suit being handed on. It is most likely highly tied up with the education and possibly scientific world where it needs to be nurtured by like-minded academics if it is to succeed long-term.
Game Changer	It is possible that the next generation could share your passion for your cause and be equally interested in carrying on the business into the long term.

It is worth making a comparison between a generational family business and a family stately home. In most cases the current family member will understand that they are purely the guardian of the estate while they reside there. It is not theirs to do with as they please for personal gain, but rather they are the custodians to preserve and protect the estate for the next generation.

So it is with family businesses. Whether you have inherited the business, or you are starting out to create a generational business, you are protecting what has gone before but you are also examining new ways to generate future income and security. You are responsible for building value for the next generation and leaving it in good shape to move forward. This is an unusual approach for many of us as we are more accustomed to a fast environment with the expectation of quick returns. To build a successful generational business, firstly you need to invest in your own knowledge and understanding of family businesses. Secondly, you need to invest in the succession.

Back to the comparison to the owner of the family estate – this scenario is fairly straightforward. Historically it is the firstborn who is expected to take on the mantle of ownership and this was developed primarily to make it clear who the successor was going to be. As the leader of a generational business, it is not so simple I'm afraid. You need to be looking at your succession planning fairly early on in your reign, so that you can support others to take on the mantle. We have discussed earlier the poor survival rate into the third generation of family businesses in the West and I want to ponder on that for a second. My own theory is that this happens because the current generation chooses its successor on the basis of the family hierarchy rather than the person who best fits the roles. Selecting a successor is always going to be a difficult position for anyone – you may be choosing between sons and daughters; whatever way you look at it there are likely to be very difficult decisions. Unlike the family owner of the estate, you have choices to make and, as a rule of thumb, the only way you can view this for the successful survival of the business is to choose the best person for the job and to think on this early on in your reign so that you can work on preparing the individuals.

Case in Point

I once worked with a sole trader who had just set up an engineering company. He grew up with a family business, but had no interest in getting involved in its leadership. After undertaking an engineering degree, he was unable to find work near his home place, a rural village where he wanted to live and work. He was also clearly a businessperson, a Lifer – and was keen to run his own show. By this stage he had tried selling cheap household products on the high street and a printing company out of the same premises. When neither of these got as far as the growth stage he gave up on the idea and moved on. By this stage he also had a young son and daughter. When I first started to work with him we spent time trying to decide what he ultimately wanted out of his business and it became clear that he wanted to hand a thriving entity to his children, to enable them to also live in their hometown if they so wished. This was a complete revelation to him and completely changed the way he saw his business. Rather than looking for the quick returns that had hampered his last attempts, he started to understand longevity in business. The business is now well established in the local community, having reached maturity, and his daughter has just come on board to run a new design division in the business to look at new product development.

TIPS AND IDEAS

A generational business can be operated by an Executive Identity other than the Descendant and should not be ignored as an option for either the Lifer or the Hobbyist as an exit strategy.

BUILDING THE BUSINESS FOR A MANAGEMENT BUY-OUT

An MBO, as it says, is when the management in a company take on the ownership of the business from you, the existing owner. This can operate in one of two ways, either involving senior staff taking equity share over time or a group of senior managers buying the business outright. As set out in Figure 10.3, this exit strategy can really be adopted by any of the Executive Identities other than those that are focused on a lifestyle business.

Figure 10.3

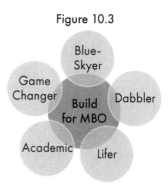

Executive Identity	Rationale
Blue-Skyer	Shareholders are part and parcel of your business. Offering shareholding to staff to ensure their loyalty to the business is not unusual for the Blue-Skyer and so an MBO is completely feasible as your exit strategy.
Descendant	The shareholding in the business tends to sit with the family members and remain with the family members. It is a difficult one for 'outsiders' to either want or try to buy into.
Hobbyist	In most cases you operate as a sole trader and even if you don't, given that the business exists because of you, there really isn't a lot for anyone else to buy into.
Dabbler	In the same way that you are willing to sell your business ventures, you are also willing to eventually sell out your shares. Again, you are likely to encourage key staff to buy into the shareholding of the business to maintain their interest and loyalty. Especially if you are involved in an industry where your knowledge and experience is weak.
Lifer	You are in business to grow a successful venture so encouraging your key staff to buy into the shareholding can be an important option for your exit strategy. Eventually they will buy you out.
Progressor	The business is really led by you and possibly another business partner. There will be enough to sustain that but not a lot more than can be bought into.
Academic	Like the Blue-Skyer you are hoping to have a tangible, sellable product on the marketplace and letting other staff members buy into the dream can secure financing to expand the business that might not otherwise be available.
Game Changer	We only need to look at funding platforms like Crowdfunding to see how suitable your business is for others; it makes sense to allow staff to buy shareholding and eventually buy you out.

In any of these Executive Identities you can potentially build a senior management team in the business and there is then a group of managers who want to become the new business leaders. Although the Dabbler can also create a lifestyle business, it is equally relevant that an MBO business can be developed, albeit the strategy from day one is very different. For any business leader, building a business for an MBO is a road with many twists and turns, and demands the business to work its way through the business life cycle, growing in revenue and employees to maturity and ready for at least the first reinvention by the new owners.

Often existing managers work over a period of time to take equity share in the business, instead of all their renumeration through salary. This type of exit strategy is common in accountancy, law, architect and consultancy firms. Those who are increasing their ownership in the business over time have an increasing say in how the business operates and therefore aim to protect their long-term investment.

The business can undergo a total change of ownership to the management team from the existing business leader and this is usually implemented over a relatively short period of time, perhaps a year or 18-month period. As a business leader this can offer many advantages. The most obvious is that it allows for a smooth transition of ownership from you to your managers. Since the new owners know the company, there is reduced risk of failure going forward and other employees, existing suppliers, financiers and other key stakeholders are reassured that there is a continuation of the status quo.

Again, this exit strategy has its own unique requirements. It means that from an early point in the decision you will need to be open and transparent with your management team. If they are going to take on ownership, they need to know that the business is on a sound footing with future growth potential. If the approach is a full MBO then it is very important that you don't neglect the day-to-day operations of the business in your keenness to work on the buyout.

TIPS AND IDEAS

MBOs can go awry in the eleventh hour, especially where there is a group of people involved. It is therefore very important to keep leading your business onwards and upwards during the preparation process, enabling the business to create your lifestyle to ultimately shut it down and move on.

A BUSINESS TO MAINTAIN A LIFESTYLE

There is a difference between a lifestyle business and all the other options open to you. The purpose of building a lifestyle business is to allow you to enjoy a particular lifestyle. As set out in Figure 10.4, this exit strategy is specific to those Executive Identities that are focused on creating a lifestyle with your business. Interestingly, the Dabbler is the one Executive Identity that can legitimately stagger either of these strategies depending on the objectives of the business leader.

Figure 10.4

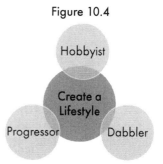

Executive Identity	Rationale
Blue-Skyer	This is a business that continually needs reinvention, either through new product development or new approaches. It does not lend itself to creating a steady lifestyle income.
Descendant	If this business does not get reinvented, it will decline and die. The fact that it needs to keep going long-term means it continually needs reinvestment and reinvention, making it fairly unsuitable for a lifestyle business.
Hobbyist	The issue is that this business needs to generate enough profit to create a lifestyle. If it can, then it could make an ideal lifestyle business.
Dabbler	Adding to your income is an important reason why you can be in business and so substituting your lifestyle is a viable exit strategy for you.
Lifer	This does not tend to be your focus for setting up in business, although it can be where you end up if you do not reinvent the business or sell out at the best time to maximise your returns.
Progressor	The business is really about creating a lifestyle for you and so this is the most common exit strategy for you at the outset.
Academic	Your business tends to be all about commercialisation and the high risks associated with that process. It is difficult to see how this could be a viable exit strategy.
Game Changer	The highs and lows created in a business trying to create a recognisable brand are not usually suitable to a lifestyle business.

Most businesses are built on the basis of maximising profits and it is often difficult as a business leader to reach a work–life balance as there's always something more to do, whether that's finding new customers, recruiting more staff or adding to product design. Whereas a lifestyle business is about creating just enough revenue so that you can sustain the lifestyle of your choice and have enough time on your hands to do the things you enjoy doing. Lifestyle business leaders tend to be calmer and less stressed, as they will only take on the level and detail of work that they wish to do – and usually the minimum to create the income they require. The downside is there really isn't any business of any value at the end of the process and so the real exit strategy for you is to close, lock the door and walk away. The business has done what it was designed to do and for that reason it has been a success.

Case in Point

Some types of business lend themselves better to a lifestyle business than others. It would be difficult, for example, to set up a computer manufacturing company as a lifestyle business due to the high level of capital investment required, but others in the service and creative industries less so. One of the classic lifestyle businesses is created when a parent wants to spend more time with family. In this scenario the employee leaves the system behind and starts working remotely and for themselves, and can therefore juggle their working life around family life.

TIPS AND IDEAS

Ensure your business idea lends itself to a lifestyle exit strategy. This strategy lends itself to the service sector and creative industries, like a photographer or graphic designer. When there is a lot of capital investment and complicated production processes, then it will be difficult to operate this business as a lifestyle venture.

KNOWING WHEN IT'S OVER – THE WARNING SIGNS

Throughout your business leadership, you hope you will naturally exit your business according to your exit strategy as set out earlier in this chapter. Sadly, this is not always the case and there are circumstances, markets, management or a lack of finance that can mean this is not a possibility. If this is the case, there are a few signs you should be aware of and know when a business is coming to an end, whether it is part of your exit plan or not. These are not to be ignored in the hope that they will go away and things will change. Watch out for the warning signs and move swiftly. It is important that you make decisions based on the business failing, not in the hope that it will turn around, and as such you are not exposed to unnecessary difficulties. Accept the reality and try to move away from the business in a logical way, one step at a time.

Outside of some of the obvious business issues that I will address later in this section, there are some really telling signs for you as a business leader that your business is starting to come to an end. One of the main red flags is when the business just becomes too much for you. When a business is failing the stress and pressure that you feel under can be overbearing. You are tired, not from a hard day's work but from an inability to plan day-to-day, let alone strategically. The tiredness you once felt from an enthusiastic day full of creativity is not what is happening now. Your business in this space is likely not even surviving, and thriving is a distant memory. To save the business you are putting in longer hours with no real returns.

It is likely that the negativity of the daily grind has also started seeping into your personal life, relationships and maybe even your health. If you believe you are in this space, then let me take you back to when you started out in business. Close your eyes and remember the excitement and thrill you once felt with the thought of making a success of your business. If your business is coming to an end it is very likely all of that has gone and you no longer take any enjoyment from what you are doing. There is an emptiness that just won't be shaken off. You are also probably struggling to get even the smallest of tasks done.

Apart from what is happening for your business leadership, the business itself is not performing in any positive way. It has lost its spark and creativity, and it is difficult for either you or your employees to keep the focus on why you are in business. Any business is there to address a problem in the marketplace and meet the needs of the customer. If you value your product more than the opinion of your customers, then they will vote with their feet and stop buying. It is very likely that with our fast-moving technology what you started out with as a business idea is just not working anymore and without the reinvention that was needed some time ago, the business is not able to survive.

Without sounding too dramatic and sparing a thought for the *Mary Celeste* and those who needed to abandon a sinking ship, when some of your key staff start to leave the business in quick succession its usually a sign that there are a few holes in the hull and they may feel it is time to bail out. When others are verifying your thinking by their actions then please take note. Letting go of a business that has been an integral part of your life, that you have nurtured from the beginning, or has been in your family for generations, is not to be underestimated.

The fuel of business is money and a business needs fuel – fact. No grey areas or maybes. If there is not enough money to deliver on your business objectives, it's just not going anywhere. How much is needed should also not be a guessing game. I have always been mystified at the number of small business leaders I have met who will openly admit they have little to no knowledge of finance. This is across the spectrum from new start-ups to seasoned business leaders. Just think, apart from the huge implications of taking a best guesstimate, how does that make you appear in your business network? You are starting out in business with a 'rough' idea of how much you might need? Not great optics! As the saying goes, if I had a pound/cent/dime for every business leader who tells me they're not sure about finance, I'd be very rich by now! How are you going to run a business if you don't understand finance? Relying on others like an accountant is not good enough, so it's time to educate yourself and fast.

Blue-Skyers should be especially self-aware. I have worked with many inventors and they all have one thing in abundance – passion for their idea. As inventors you are engrossed in the commercialisation of your invention. You are focusing totally on making your concept into a product that can be sold and you are passionate about how big your idea can get. Logically, in your view, without a product there can be no business! To a certain extent this is true. Yet, without bringing the financial backing along with your invention, your idea will reach a brick wall with nowhere to go. Sure, secure your IP if need be, line up the ducks, but get your financial interest secured early in the conceptual stage. Make sure all your hard work is not in vain.

Case in Point

I had the challenge of working with an engineering design company a few years ago. The entrepreneur, a Blue-Skyer, ended up in my training room having worked on his bicycle invention for three years. With a prototype developed he had recently given up his well-paid job to totally concentrate on his venture and bring the product to market. So far, the story was not unusual and has taken a path that many have travelled. With some probing, however, it was clear that there was no business plan in place and no finance to fund the next (expensive) stage in the process – commercialisation. With no income and a guestimate of commercialisation costs at €100k, we quickly got down to putting together concrete cash flow forecasts and a lot of hiking around funders. Some would say he put unnecessary stress on himself by putting the cart before the horse. I must say, I tend to agree!

TIPS AND IDEAS

Educate yourself on business finance. Learn to read a set of accounts, understand a cash flow forecast, and above all set up a management accounting system from day one so that you can see how your business is operating financially from a robust just-in-time financial system. What I mean is making sure you have spreadsheets and software that shows you exactly where your money is on a daily basis – in the bank, with debtors or tied up with creditors. Understand that a set of accounts completed by your accountant once a year is only a photograph of your situation on that date. They are actually out of date the day after they are produced.

The time needed for a business to turn a net profit will vary from one industry to another and from one business to another. When the business is not meeting the quarterly requirement to breakeven and if you continue too long on this road, you could end up with personal debt as well as business debt. There is no point in prolonging the agony.

SUMMARY EXERCISE

If you have not already done so, then it is time to decide on the exit strategy for your business. To do this there are four questions you need to answer.

1. What do you finally plan to do with your business?
2. How do you intend to exit the business?
3. When do you want to exit your business?
4. What actions do you need to take to achieve 1–3?

In Summary

I really do believe that you should set your exit strategy at the outset and, in that way, you always know where you are going. You are not Christopher Columbus exploring new lands; you are a business leader who needs to have a clear vision for yourself and others. There is no denying that your Executive Identity will dictate that vision to a large extent. Your Executive Identity is particularly suited to some exit strategies more than others and it will be supportive to know what these are and therefore what your 'easier' options are. If you are reading this book and you are well into the establishment of your business, then at least fix your exit strategy from this day forward.

AFTERWORD

In all my years of working with business leaders I have applied these ideas and concepts, and I believe they work. This book should provide you with a lot to think about in your business leadership. I hope you have been given an insight that you didn't have before you started reading.

It is now over to you to start your journey and decide what you do with what you have read. Think about the key points you have learned and decide how you will apply them to understanding your own business leadership:

✓ Building a business is influenced by what you are – your Executive Identity – more than any other factor.

✓ As a business leader you will have a main Executive Identity, either as a lifelong attachment or a moving factor as you change your career. What is yours?

✓ Your Executive Identity will have characteristics and leadership styles that are unique, and can supply you with strengths and opportunities but also ask you to address your weaknesses and threats.

✓ Understand where you might get stuck in the business life cycle and try to propel yourself forward in your thinking, decisions and risk-taking.

✓ Appreciate the domineering influences on your management functions and what that means in your business leadership.

✓ Some Executive Identities work better together than others in business partnerships, teams and boards of directors. Working towards a collaborative mix on each of these will support the success of your business leadership.

✓ It is useful to identify your support team and make it work for you regardless of the stage of growth of your business.

✓ Work at maximising your efforts for the biggest gains and let go of the things that are making you a 'busy fool'.

✓ Looking after yourself is not a luxury, but rather a necessity for strong business growth.
✓ Know what you want out of your venture before you start and then keep that vision as you move through the business life cycle.
✓ Just remember you can make your own luck in business leadership!

CONTACT THE AUTHOR

If you have been inspired by my book and are interested in learning more about its content, or the unique form of business coaching I provide, then please get in touch at https://michellelestas.com/contact-details/. If you have found parts of the book particularly inspiring then please leave a review at https://michellelestas.com/identity-led-business-growth/.

Notes

1. Ridley, M. (2004) *Nature via Nurture: Genes, Experience and What Makes Us Human*, HarperPerennial.
2. Tajfel, H. and Turner, J.C. (1979) 'An Integrative Theory of Intergroup Conflict' in Austin, W.G. and Worchel, S. (eds.), *The Social Psychology of Intergroup Relations*, Monterey, CA: Brooks-Cole 33–47.
3. Smilor, R., Gibson, D. and Dietrich, G. (1990) 'University Spin-Out Companies: Technology Start-Ups from UT-Austin' in *Journal of Business Venturing*, 5(1) 63–76.
4. Mansfield, M. (2019) 'Startup Statistics – The Numbers You Need to Know' in *Startup*, 40, 28 March 2019.
5. McLeod, S.A. (2017) 'Type A Personality', retrieved from https://www.simply psychology.org/personality.
6. Maslow, A.H. (1943) 'A Theory of Human Motivation', in *Psychological Review*, 50, 370–396.
7. The answer is:

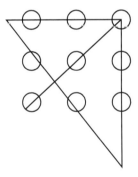

8. Charlebois, S. (2019) 'Beyond Meat Owns the Plant-Based Meat Market, for Now', in *Canadian Grocer*, 25 April 2019.

9 Denver, J. (1985), 'The Harder They Fall', *Dreamland Express*.

10 *The Morecambe Guardian*, November 1931.

11 Collins, J. and Hansen, M. (2011) *Great by Choice: Uncertainty, Chaos, and Luck—Why Some Thrive Despite Them All*, HarperBusiness.

12 https://en.wikipedia.org/wiki/Pareto_principle.

13 Office for National Statistics, 2017.

14 https://workplaceinsight.net/many-uk-freelancers-feel-lonely-and-isolated-following-leap-to-self-employment.

15 Lewis, L. (2001) *Managing Business and Service Networks*, Springer, p. 138.

16 https://en.wikipedia.org/wiki/C._Northcote_Parkinson.

17 https://www.toolshero.com/personal-development/eisenhower-matrix.